A Healthy Living Book

Crafted by Skriuwer

Table of Contents

Chapter 6: Healthy Relationships

- 6.1 The Impact of Relationships on Health
- 6.2 Building Strong Relationships
- 6.3 Setting Boundaries
- 6.4 Managing Conflict in Relationships
- 6.5 The Role of Community in Health

Chapter 7: Work-Life Balance

- 7.1 The Importance of Balance Between Work and Life
- 7.2 Strategies for Achieving Balance
- 7.3 Dealing with Burnout
- 7.4 The Role of Leisure and Hobbies
- 7.5 Maintaining Balance During Life Changes

Chapter 8: The Role of Preventive Health

- 8.1 Understanding Preventive Health
- 8.2 Regular Health Screenings
- 8.3 Vaccinations and Immunizations
- 8.4 Preventive Dental Care
- 8.5 Developing a Personalized Health Plan

Chapter 9: Environmental Factors and Health

- 9.1 The Impact of Your Environment on Health
- 9.2 Creating a Healthy Home Environment
- 9.3 Reducing Exposure to Toxins
- 9.4 The Role of Nature in Health
- 9.5 Sustainable Living for Health

Chapter 10: Healthy Aging

- 10.1 Understanding the Aging Process
- 10.2 Nutrition for Healthy Aging
- 10.3 Maintaining Physical Activity in Older Age
- 10.4 Mental Health and Aging
- 10.5 Social Connections in Later Life

Chapter 11: The Role of Technology in Health

- 11.1 Health Technology Overview
- 11.2 Fitness Trackers and Apps
- 11.3 Telemedicine and Online Health Resources
- 11.4 The Impact of Screen Time on Health
- 11.5 Future Trends in Health Technology

Chapter 12: Cultivating Healthy Habits

- 12.1 The Science of Habit Formation
- 12.2 Breaking Unhealthy Habits
- 12.3 Developing New Healthy Habits
- 12.4 The Role of Motivation and Willpower
- 12.5 Tracking Progress and Celebrating Success

Chapter 13: Holistic Health Approaches

- 13.1 What is Holistic Health?
- 13.2 Integrating Mind, Body, and Spirit
- 13.3 Alternative and Complementary Therapies
- 13.4 The Role of Nutrition in Holistic Health
- 13.5 Creating a Personal Holistic Health Plan

Chapter 14: The Importance of Self-Care

- 14.1 What is Self-Care?
- 14.2 Incorporating Self-Care into Daily Life
- 14.3 The Role of Self-Compassion in Self-Care
- 14.4 Self-Care for Mental Health
- 14.5 Overcoming Barriers to Self-Care

Chapter 15: Conclusion and Moving Forward

- 15.1 Recap of Key Takeaways
- 15.2 Developing a Personal Health Plan
- 15.3 Staying Committed to a Healthy Lifestyle
- 15.4 Resources for Continued Learning
- 15.5 Final Words of Encouragement

Chapter 1

Understanding Healthy Living

Defining Healthy Living

Healthy living encompasses a holistic approach to well-being that integrates physical, mental, and emotional health. It is not a one-size-fits-all concept; rather, it is a personalized journey that reflects individual choices, lifestyles, and goals. At its core, healthy living is about making informed decisions that enhance quality of life, longevity, and overall happiness.

Physical Health: The Foundation of Healthy Living

Physical health is often the most visible aspect of healthy living. It involves regular physical activity, balanced nutrition, adequate sleep, and routine preventive health care. Engaging in regular exercise helps to maintain a healthy weight, reduces the risk of chronic diseases, and enhances cardiovascular health. It is recommended that adults engage in at least 150 minutes of moderate aerobic activity or 75 minutes of vigorous activity each week, complemented by strength training exercises on two or more days a week.

Nutrition plays a pivotal role in physical health. A balanced diet that includes a variety of fruits, vegetables, whole grains, lean proteins, and healthy fats provides essential nutrients that fuel the body and support optimal functioning. Understanding the principles of nutrition, including the significance of macronutrients and micronutrients, empowers individuals to make healthier food choices that cater to their specific needs.

Mental and Emotional Well-Being: A Critical Component

While physical health is crucial, mental and emotional well-being is equally important in defining healthy living. Mental health influences how we think, feel, and act, and it affects our ability to handle stress, relate to others, and make choices. Practices such as mindfulness, meditation, and cognitive behavioral strategies can enhance mental resilience, improve mood, and reduce anxiety.

Emotional well-being involves recognizing and managing our feelings, building self-esteem, and fostering positive relationships. Developing emotional intelligence helps individuals navigate the complexities of interpersonal dynamics, leading to healthier connections and improved overall satisfaction in life.

The Interconnectedness of Health Dimensions

Healthy living recognizes the interconnectedness of physical, mental, and emotional health. For instance, regular physical activity has been shown to reduce symptoms of anxiety and depression, demonstrating the profound impact that exercise can have on mental well-being. Conversely, poor mental health can lead to unhealthy lifestyle choices, such as poor eating habits or inactivity, creating a cycle that can be difficult to break.

Additionally, social connections play a vital role in healthy living. A strong support network can provide emotional support, foster a sense of belonging, and encourage healthy behaviors. Engaging in community activities and nurturing relationships can enhance mental and emotional health, reinforcing the idea that healthy living is not just an individual pursuit but a collective endeavor.

Embracing Balance and Personalization

Defining healthy living also involves embracing balance. It is essential to find harmony between various aspects of life, including work, relationships, leisure, and self-care. Striking this balance prevents burnout and promotes sustained well-being.

Moreover, healthy living is inherently personal. What works for one individual may not be suitable for another. Personal preferences, cultural practices, and individual circumstances must be considered when defining a healthy lifestyle. This personalization encourages individuals to take ownership of their health journey, making choices that resonate with their values and aspirations.

In conclusion, defining healthy living is an intricate interplay of physical, mental, and emotional health. It is about making informed lifestyle choices, fostering connections, and embracing balance while recognizing the individual nature of each person's journey. By understanding and implementing these principles, individuals can cultivate a fulfilling and vibrant life that reflects their unique definition of health.

The Benefits of Healthy Living

Living a healthy life offers a myriad of benefits that extend beyond the mere absence of disease or illness. The concept of healthy living encompasses a holistic approach that includes physical fitness, mental acuity, and emotional well-being. Each of these facets is intricately connected and contributes to an improved quality of life. Here, we delve into the various advantages that arise from adopting a healthy lifestyle.

Physical Advantages

First and foremost, the physical benefits of healthy living are perhaps the most evident. Engaging in regular physical activity, maintaining a balanced diet, and ensuring adequate hydration contribute significantly to one's physical health.

1. Improved Cardiovascular Health: Regular exercise strengthens the heart, improves circulation, and lowers blood pressure. This, in turn, reduces the risk of heart disease, stroke, and other cardiovascular conditions.

2. Weight Management: A healthy lifestyle helps in maintaining a healthy weight. Consuming nutrient-dense foods and engaging in physical activity allows individuals to manage their body weight effectively, reducing the risk of obesity-related diseases such as diabetes and hypertension.

3. Enhanced Immune Function: Proper nutrition, regular exercise, and adequate rest bolster the immune system, making the body more resilient against infections and illnesses.

4. Increased Longevity: Studies have shown that individuals who adhere to a healthy lifestyle tend to live longer, healthier lives. By reducing the risk of chronic diseases, healthy living can extend both life expectancy and quality of life.

Mental Advantages

The mental benefits of healthy living are equally significant. A balanced lifestyle fosters cognitive function and mental clarity, contributing to overall mental health.

1. Enhanced Cognitive Function: Regular physical activity has been linked to improved brain health, including enhanced memory, sharper thinking, and better problem-solving skills. Exercise increases blood flow to the brain, promoting the growth of new neurons and improving synaptic plasticity.

2. Reduction in Anxiety and Depression: Engaging in physical activity releases endorphins, often referred to as "feel-good" hormones, which can help alleviate feelings of anxiety and depression. Additionally, healthy eating patterns, particularly those rich in omega-3 fatty acids and antioxidants, can positively influence mood and cognitive function.

3. Increased Focus and Productivity: A well-nourished body and mind can lead to improved concentration and productivity. Healthy living encourages better sleep patterns and energy levels, which are essential for maintaining focus throughout the day.

Emotional Advantages

The emotional benefits of healthy living cannot be overstated. A holistic approach promotes emotional resilience and stability.

1. Improved Self-Esteem and Body Image: Engaging in healthy behaviors often leads to improved physical appearance and fitness levels, which can boost self-esteem and body image. This positive self-perception can significantly enhance emotional well-being.

2. Stress Management: Healthy living incorporates practices such as mindfulness, meditation, and regular physical activity, which are effective in managing stress. These practices help individuals cultivate a calm state of mind, allowing for better emotional regulation.

3. Stronger Relationships: A healthy lifestyle often encourages social interactions, whether through group exercise classes, community engagement, or shared meals. Strong social connections are vital for emotional support and overall happiness.

4. Resilience: Adopting a healthy lifestyle fosters emotional resilience, helping individuals cope with life's challenges more effectively. This resilience can be attributed to a greater sense of control over one's health, leading to improved problem-solving skills and adaptability.

In conclusion, the benefits of healthy living extend far beyond physical health. Embracing a holistic approach that encompasses physical, mental, and emotional well-being leads to a more fulfilling and vibrant life. By understanding and applying these principles, individuals can significantly enhance their overall quality of life, paving the way for long-term health and happiness.

Common Misconceptions About Health

In the pursuit of a healthy lifestyle, individuals often encounter a myriad of myths and misconceptions that can cloud their understanding of what it truly means to live healthily. These misunderstandings can lead to misguided practices and, ultimately, hinder one's health journey. Here, we will explore some of the most prevalent misconceptions about health and provide clarity to help individuals make informed choices.

1. Myth: All fats are bad for you.

A common belief is that dietary fat should be entirely avoided to maintain a healthy lifestyle. However, this is a misconception. Fat is an essential macronutrient that plays a crucial role in the body, including supporting cell structure, hormone production, and the absorption of fat-soluble vitamins (A, D, E, and K). It is important to distinguish between unhealthy trans fats and saturated fats found in processed foods, and healthy fats present in foods such as avocados, nuts, seeds, and olive oil. Emphasizing healthy fats in moderation can contribute positively to overall health.

2. Myth: You can spot-reduce fat.

Many believe that they can target specific areas of their body to lose fat through localized exercises, such as doing countless crunches to eliminate belly fat. However, spot reduction is a myth. Fat loss occurs across the entire body through a combination of overall caloric deficit and physical activity. A comprehensive approach that includes cardiovascular exercise, strength training, and a balanced diet is necessary for effective fat loss.

3. Myth: Carbs are the enemy.

The notion that carbohydrates are detrimental to health has gained traction, particularly with the rise of low-carb diets. Yet, carbohydrates are a primary source of energy for the body and critical for brain function. The key is to focus on the quality of carbohydrates consumed. Whole grains, fruits, and vegetables provide essential nutrients and fiber, while processed sugars and refined grains should be limited. A balanced diet includes healthy carbohydrates that support sustained energy levels.

4. Myth: You need to exercise vigorously to be healthy.

Another widespread misconception is that only high-intensity workouts can produce health benefits. In reality, any physical activity can contribute to overall health. The key is consistency and finding forms of exercise that one enjoys. Moderate activities such as walking, gardening, or yoga can significantly improve cardiovascular health, flexibility, and mental well-being. The important takeaway is that movement, regardless of intensity, is beneficial.

5. Myth: Mental health issues are a sign of weakness.

Mental health is often shrouded in stigma, leading many to believe that experiencing mental health challenges indicates personal weakness. This misconception undermines the reality that mental health issues can affect anyone, regardless of strength or resilience. Mental health is just as important as physical health, and seeking help or support is a sign of strength, not weakness. Promoting open conversations about mental health can encourage more individuals to seek the help they need.

6. Myth: Supplements can replace a healthy diet.

While vitamins and supplements can play a role in filling nutritional gaps, they cannot substitute for a balanced diet rich in whole foods. The body benefits from the complex interplay of nutrients found in fruits, vegetables, whole grains, and lean proteins, which cannot be replicated in pill form. A healthy diet should be prioritized, with supplements used only as an adjunct to a well-rounded nutritional plan.

Conclusion

Debunking these common misconceptions about health is crucial for fostering a more accurate understanding of what it means to live a healthy life. By educating ourselves and others, we can dispel myths and encourage healthier choices rooted in evidence-based practices. Awareness is the first step toward building a sustainable, healthy lifestyle that prioritizes both physical and mental well-being.

Assessing Your Current Lifestyle

Assessing your current lifestyle is a crucial first step toward achieving a healthier life. By understanding your habits, routines, and behaviors, you can identify areas for improvement and make informed decisions about your health journey. This evaluation requires a comprehensive approach, examining various aspects of your daily life, including nutrition, physical activity, mental well-being, sleep, and social connections.

1. Journaling Your Habits

One effective method to assess your current lifestyle is to keep a detailed journal for at least one week. Document your daily activities, meals, exercise routines, sleep patterns, and emotional states. Recording this information helps you recognize trends and patterns that might otherwise go unnoticed. Look for areas where you may be excelling, as well as aspects that could use improvement.

For instance, note the amount of fruits and vegetables you consume daily, your water intake, the frequency and intensity of your physical activity, and your sleep duration and quality. Additionally, document how you feel emotionally and mentally throughout the week. This holistic view will provide valuable insights into your lifestyle choices.

2. Evaluating Nutrition

Nutrition plays a significant role in overall health. After journaling your food intake, analyze your diet for balance and variety. Are you consuming adequate amounts of macronutrients (carbohydrates, proteins, and fats) and micronutrients (vitamins and minerals)? A well-rounded diet should include whole foods such as fruits, vegetables, lean proteins, whole grains, and healthy fats while minimizing processed foods high in sugar and unhealthy fats.

Consider using online tools or apps that provide nutritional analysis of your meals, helping you identify deficiencies or excesses in your diet. Additionally, reflect on your eating habits: do you eat mindfully, or do you often engage in emotional eating or distractions during meals? Recognizing these behaviors is essential for fostering a healthier relationship with food.

3. Analyzing Physical Activity

Physical activity is vital for maintaining physical health and emotional well-being. Reflect on your current exercise routine: how often do you engage in physical activity, and what types of exercises do you perform? The CDC recommends at least 150 minutes of moderate aerobic activity each week, along with strength training exercises on two or more days.

Evaluate your fitness level by considering your endurance, strength, flexibility, and balance. Do you enjoy your current activities, or do you find them tedious? Finding enjoyable forms of exercise not only boosts adherence but also enhances the overall experience of staying active.

4. Assessing Mental and Emotional Health

Mental health is as crucial as physical health. Reflect on your emotional well-being and stress levels. Are you often overwhelmed, anxious, or depressed? Consider the coping mechanisms you use when faced with stress—do they promote health, or do they lead to unhealthy habits such as overeating, substance use, or social withdrawal?

Engaging in self-reflection practices, such as mindfulness or therapy, can help you better understand your mental state and develop healthier coping strategies. It's also beneficial to evaluate your social connections. Healthy relationships can greatly influence your emotional health, so consider the quality of your interactions with family, friends, and coworkers.

5. Reviewing Sleep Patterns

Sleep is critical for overall health, yet many overlook its importance. Assess your sleep quality by asking yourself whether you consistently get the recommended 7-9 hours of sleep each night and whether you feel rested upon waking. Keep track of your sleep habits, including bedtime routines and sleep environment. If you struggle with sleep, consider factors that may be contributing, such as screen time, caffeine intake, or stress.

Conclusion

Assessing your current lifestyle is an empowering process that lays the groundwork for meaningful change. By taking a comprehensive look at your habits, you can identify strengths and areas for growth, ultimately leading you toward a healthier, more balanced life. Remember, this evaluation is not a one-time task but an ongoing process that evolves as you progress on your health journey.

The Role of Balance in Health

Balance is a fundamental principle in the pursuit of a healthy lifestyle, encompassing not just the physical aspects of health but also mental, emotional, and social dimensions. Achieving balance means finding harmony among various facets of life, which can greatly enhance overall well-being and lead to a more fulfilling existence. This section delves into the various dimensions of balance and its significance in promoting health.

1. Physical Balance

Physical balance refers to the equilibrium between different types of physical activities and rest. Engaging in exercise is crucial for maintaining physical health; however, excessive exercise without adequate rest can lead to fatigue, injuries, and burnout. Conversely, a sedentary lifestyle can lead to a host of health issues, including obesity, heart disease, and weakened muscles. The key is to integrate various forms of physical activity, such as aerobic exercises, strength training, flexibility workouts, and rest days, to create a well-rounded fitness regimen. This approach not only optimizes physical health but also enhances mood and energy levels.

2. Mental and Emotional Balance

Mental and emotional balance involves managing stress, emotions, and mental health effectively. In today's fast-paced world, individuals often neglect their mental health in favor of work or social obligations. This imbalance can lead to anxiety, depression, and other mental health issues. Strategies such as mindfulness, meditation, and positive thinking are essential in fostering mental resilience. By prioritizing emotional well-being and incorporating practices that promote relaxation and reflection, individuals can better navigate life's challenges and maintain a positive outlook.

3. Social Balance

Social connections are paramount for mental and emotional health. However, the quality of these relationships matters significantly. Balancing time among family, friends, and community involvement can foster a supportive network that enhances feelings of belonging and security. Conversely, toxic relationships can drain emotional resources and lead to stress. Setting boundaries and recognizing when to distance oneself from unhealthy dynamics is crucial in maintaining social balance. Engaging in community activities can also enrich one's social life, providing opportunities for connection and support.

4. Work-Life Balance

Achieving a healthy work-life balance is increasingly challenging in a world that prizes productivity. Overworking can lead to burnout, decreased productivity, and physical health issues. It is essential to delineate boundaries between work and personal time. This can involve setting specific work hours, taking regular breaks, and ensuring time is allocated for leisure and hobbies. Maintaining this balance contributes to overall happiness, reduces stress, and can even improve work performance.

5. Lifestyle Balance

Lastly, balance in lifestyle choices—such as nutrition, physical activity, and leisure activities—is critical. A balanced diet that includes a variety of nutrients supports physical health and energy levels. Similarly, balancing leisure activities with responsibilities helps prevent burnout and enriches one's life experience. Engaging in hobbies and interests outside of work can promote creativity, relaxation, and personal fulfillment.

Conclusion

In summary, balance is a foundational element of healthy living that encompasses physical, mental, emotional, social, and lifestyle aspects. It is essential to recognize that achieving balance is not a one-time effort but an ongoing process that requires self-awareness, reflection, and adaptability. By consciously striving for balance in all areas of life, individuals can enhance their overall health and well-being, leading to a more vibrant and fulfilling existence. As we navigate the complexities of modern life, fostering balance can empower us to live healthier, happier lives.

Chapter 2

Nutrition for a Healthy Life

The Basics of Nutrition

Nutrition is a cornerstone of healthy living, playing a crucial role in maintaining overall health and well-being. At the heart of nutrition are two categories of nutrients: macronutrients and micronutrients. Understanding these nutrients is essential for building a balanced diet that supports your body's needs.

Macronutrients: The Energy Providers

Macronutrients are the nutrients that provide the energy necessary for our bodies to function. They include carbohydrates, proteins, and fats, each serving unique roles in health.

1. Carbohydrates: Often referred to as the body's primary source of energy, carbohydrates can be categorized into simple and complex forms. Simple carbohydrates, found in sugars and processed foods, provide quick energy but can lead to spikes in blood sugar levels. In contrast, complex carbohydrates, such as whole grains, fruits, and vegetables, offer more sustained energy, fiber, and essential vitamins and minerals. Incorporating complex carbohydrates into your diet is crucial for maintaining energy levels and supporting digestive health.

2. Proteins: Proteins are vital for growth, repair, and maintenance of body tissues. Composed of amino acids, proteins are necessary for the production of enzymes, hormones, and other body chemicals. There are two types of proteins: complete and incomplete. Complete proteins, found in animal products like meat, dairy, and eggs, contain all essential amino acids. Incomplete proteins, found in plant sources like beans, lentils, and nuts, may lack one or more essential amino acids but can be combined to form complete proteins. It's essential to include a variety of protein sources in your diet to ensure adequate amino acid intake.

3. Fats: Often misunderstood, fats are essential for various bodily functions, including hormone production, nutrient absorption, and energy storage. Fats can be categorized into saturated, unsaturated, and trans fats. Unsaturated fats, found in olive oil, avocados, and fish, are considered beneficial for heart health, while saturated fats, found in red meat and butter, should be consumed in moderation. Trans fats, often found in processed foods, should be avoided as they increase the risk of heart disease. Including healthy fats in your diet supports cognitive function and helps maintain overall health.

Micronutrients: The Vital Supporters
While macronutrients provide energy, micronutrients—vitamins and minerals—are essential for supporting numerous physiological functions and maintaining overall health.

1. Vitamins: These organic compounds are critical for metabolic processes and are divided into water-soluble (B vitamins and vitamin C) and fat-soluble (vitamins A, D, E, and K) categories. Each vitamin plays specific roles in the body, such as supporting immune function, promoting healthy skin, and aiding in the absorption of calcium. A diet rich in fruits, vegetables, whole grains, and lean proteins typically provides sufficient vitamins to meet daily requirements.

2. Minerals: Minerals are inorganic elements that contribute to various bodily functions, including bone health, fluid balance, and muscle contraction. Key minerals include calcium, potassium, iron, and magnesium. Calcium is crucial for bone strength, while iron is essential for oxygen transport in the blood. A balanced diet that includes dairy products, leafy greens, nuts, seeds, and lean meats can help ensure adequate mineral intake.

Conclusion
Understanding macronutrients and micronutrients is essential for creating a balanced diet. While macronutrients provide the energy needed for bodily functions, micronutrients support these functions and contribute to overall health. By incorporating a variety of foods from each nutrient category, individuals can cultivate a healthy lifestyle that supports physical, mental, and emotional well-being. Prioritizing whole, unprocessed foods and maintaining a balanced intake of macronutrients and micronutrients is key to achieving optimal health outcomes.

Creating a Balanced Diet
Building a balanced diet is an essential component of healthy living, as it ensures that your body receives the necessary nutrients to function optimally. A balanced diet includes a variety of foods in the right proportions, providing the essential macronutrients—carbohydrates, proteins, and fats—as well as micronutrients, such as vitamins and minerals. Here's how you can create a balanced diet that meets your nutritional needs.

1. Understand Macronutrients
Carbohydrates are the body's primary source of energy. They can be categorized into simple carbohydrates (sugars) and complex carbohydrates (starches and fibers). Aim for complex carbohydrates from whole grains, fruits, and vegetables, as they provide sustained energy along with fiber, which aids digestion.

Proteins are vital for growth, tissue repair, and the production of enzymes and hormones. Include various protein sources in your diet such as lean meats, poultry, fish, legumes, nuts, and dairy products. For those following a vegetarian or vegan diet, plant-based proteins like lentils, beans, quinoa, and tofu are excellent options.

Fats are essential for energy, hormone production, and the absorption of fat-soluble vitamins (A, D, E, K). Emphasize healthy fats found in avocados, nuts, seeds, olive oil, and fatty fish like salmon. Limit saturated fats and avoid trans fats to maintain cardiovascular health.

2. Incorporate Micronutrients
Micronutrients, including vitamins and minerals, play crucial roles in the body, from supporting immune function to bone health. A diverse diet rich in fruits and vegetables can help you meet your micronutrient needs. Aim to include a colorful variety of produce, as different colors often represent different nutrients. For instance, leafy greens are high in vitamin K, while oranges are rich in vitamin C.

3. Portion Control and Balance
To create a balanced diet, it's important to consider portion sizes. The concept of "MyPlate," developed by the USDA, can guide you in visualizing how to fill your plate. Ideally, half your plate should consist of fruits and vegetables, a quarter should be whole grains, and the remaining quarter should be protein. This model helps ensure that you're consuming a variety of food groups in appropriate amounts.

4. Meal Planning
Planning your meals in advance can help you maintain a balanced diet. Start by creating a weekly menu that includes a variety of foods from all food groups. Consider preparing larger batches of healthy meals for the week, making it easier to stick to your dietary goals. Keep healthy snacks on hand, such as fruits, nuts, or yogurt, to prevent reaching for processed options when hunger strikes.

5. Stay Hydrated
Water is often overlooked but is vital for overall health. Proper hydration aids digestion, nutrient absorption, and temperature regulation. Aim for at least eight 8-ounce glasses of water a day, adjusting for activity level and climate. Herbal teas and water-rich foods, like fruits and vegetables, can also contribute to your hydration needs.

6. Listen to Your Body
Finally, pay attention to your body's hunger and fullness cues. Eating mindfully helps you understand your nutritional needs better and prevents overeating. Take the time to enjoy your meals, chew slowly, and savor flavors. This practice not only enhances your eating experience but also supports your overall well-being.

In conclusion, creating a balanced diet requires a thoughtful approach to food selection, portion sizes, and meal planning. By focusing on a variety of nutrient-dense foods, staying hydrated, and listening to your body, you can build a diet that not only meets your nutritional needs but also supports your overall health and wellness.

The Importance of Hydration

Water is the essence of life, constituting about 60% of the human body, and plays a crucial role in maintaining overall health. Hydration, or the process of maintaining an adequate level of water in the body, is fundamental for various physiological functions, and understanding its importance is key to promoting a healthy lifestyle.

1. Essential Functions of Water in the Body

Water serves numerous vital functions in the body. It acts as a solvent, facilitating biochemical reactions and enabling nutrients to be transported and absorbed effectively. This is particularly significant in the digestive process, where water helps break down food, allowing essential nutrients to be absorbed into the bloodstream.

Moreover, water is crucial for thermoregulation. It helps regulate body temperature through sweating and respiration. When the body heats up, sweat evaporates from the skin surface, dissipating heat and cooling the body down. Dehydration can impair this process, leading to heat-related illnesses, especially in hot weather or during vigorous physical activity.

2. Impact on Physical Performance

Hydration directly impacts physical performance. Even mild dehydration can lead to fatigue, reduced endurance, and decreased coordination. Studies have shown that a loss of just 2% of body weight in fluids can impair physical performance, making hydration especially important for athletes and individuals engaging in regular exercise.

In addition to physical performance, hydration supports cardiovascular health. When adequately hydrated, blood volume and circulation can be maintained efficiently, ensuring that oxygen and nutrients reach muscles and organs effectively. Dehydration, on the other hand, can lead to increased heart rate and reduced blood flow, making the heart work harder, which is particularly concerning during intense physical exertion.

3. Cognitive and Emotional Health

Hydration also plays a critical role in cognitive function. The brain is composed of approximately 75% water, and even mild dehydration can lead to difficulties in concentration, increased perception of task difficulty, and mood swings. Research has indicated that dehydration can impair short-term memory and cognitive performance, underscoring the importance of maintaining adequate fluid intake for mental clarity and emotional stability.

Moreover, water consumption is linked to emotional well-being. Many individuals experience irritability and mood disturbances when dehydrated. Staying hydrated can help stabilize mood and improve overall mental health, making it an essential component of emotional regulation.

4. Recommendations for Hydration

To maintain optimal hydration levels, it is generally recommended that adults drink at least eight 8-ounce glasses of water a day, often referred to as the "8x8 rule." However, individual hydration needs may vary based on factors such as age, activity level, climate, and overall health.

In addition to drinking plain water, hydration can be supported through the consumption of fruits and vegetables, many of which have high water content, such as cucumbers, oranges, and watermelon. It is also important to recognize the signs of dehydration, which include increased thirst, dry mouth, fatigue, and dark yellow urine.

5. Conclusion

In conclusion, hydration is a cornerstone of healthy living, influencing physical performance, cognitive function, and emotional well-being. By prioritizing hydration and understanding its crucial role in maintaining health, individuals can enhance their overall well-being and support their journey toward a healthier lifestyle. As we navigate through our daily activities, making a conscious effort to drink enough water and consume hydrating foods can lead to significant benefits that enhance our quality of life.

Understanding Food Labels

In an age where the food market is flooded with options, understanding food labels is essential for making informed dietary choices. Food packaging often contains a wealth of information that can help consumers determine the nutritional value and overall healthfulness of a product. Here, we will break down the key components of food labels and provide guidance on how to interpret them effectively.

1. The Nutrition Facts Panel

The Nutrition Facts panel is the cornerstone of food labeling, providing important nutritional information per serving. Here are the main elements to focus on:

- **Serving Size:** This indicates the amount of food that is considered a serving, typically measured in cups, ounces, or pieces. It's crucial to note that many people underestimate serving sizes, leading to the consumption of more calories and nutrients than intended.

- **Calories:** This figure represents the total energy provided by one serving. Understanding caloric intake is vital for managing body weight and overall health.

- **Nutrients:** The panel lists various nutrients, including macronutrients (fats, carbohydrates, and proteins) and micronutrients (vitamins and minerals). Pay attention to the following:

 - **Total Fat:** Look for types of fat. Unsaturated fats (monounsaturated and polyunsaturated) are healthier than saturated fats and trans fats, which are linked to heart disease.

 - **Sodium:** High sodium intake can lead to hypertension. Aim to choose products with lower sodium content.

 - **Total Carbohydrates:** This includes dietary fiber and sugars. Focus on foods high in fiber (5 grams or more per serving) and low in added sugars (ideally less than 10 grams).

- **% Daily Value (%DV):** This percentage indicates how much a nutrient in a serving contributes to a daily diet based on a 2,000-calorie daily intake. A value of 5% or less is considered low, while 20% or more is high. This tool helps you gauge whether a food is a good source of a nutrient.

2. Ingredients List

The ingredients list provides transparency about what is in the product. Ingredients are listed in descending order by weight, meaning the first ingredient is the most prevalent. **Here are some tips for analyzing the ingredients list:**

- **Whole Foods:** Look for whole, minimally processed ingredients. Ingredients like whole grains, fruits, and vegetables should be at the top of the list.

- **Avoid Artificial Additives:** Watch out for long lists containing artificial colors, preservatives, and flavorings. Shorter ingredient lists typically indicate a more whole-food product.

- **Allergens:** Common allergens (like nuts, dairy, soy, and gluten) are often highlighted at the end of the ingredients list. If you have food sensitivities, this section is critical.

3. Claims and Certifications

Food labels may feature various claims, such as "low fat," "organic," "gluten-free," or "high in fiber." While these claims can provide useful information, they can also be misleading. Here are a few things to consider:

- **Understanding Claims:** Familiarize yourself with the definitions of these claims. For example, "organic" means the product contains at least 95% organic ingredients, while "gluten-free" must meet FDA standards.

- Look Beyond Claims: Just because a product carries a health claim doesn't mean it's nutritionally sound. Always refer back to the Nutrition Facts panel and the ingredients list.

4. Serving Size vs. Package Size

Many packages contain multiple servings, so it's essential to be mindful of how many servings you consume in one sitting. If you eat the entire package, you must multiply the nutritional values by the number of servings to understand your intake properly.

Conclusion

Understanding food labels empowers consumers to make healthier choices and take control of their nutrition. By familiarizing yourself with the Nutrition Facts panel, ingredients list, claims, and the distinction between serving and package sizes, you can navigate the grocery aisles more confidently. This knowledge not only contributes to better health outcomes but also fosters a greater appreciation for the food you consume.

Meal Planning and Preparation

Meal planning and preparation are essential components of maintaining a healthy diet. These practices not only streamline your eating habits but also reduce the temptation to resort to unhealthy food choices. By dedicating time to plan and prepare meals in advance, you can ensure that your nutritional needs are met while also saving time and money. Here are some effective strategies for successful meal planning and preparation that can lead to consistent healthy eating.

1. Set Clear Goals

Begin by establishing clear and achievable goals for your meal planning. Ask yourself what you want to accomplish—whether it's losing weight, increasing energy levels, or simply eating more whole foods. Specific goals will help you tailor your meal plans to suit your needs. For instance, if weight loss is your goal, focus on incorporating more fruits, vegetables, and lean proteins into your meals while reducing processed foods and sugars.

2. Create a Weekly Menu

Drafting a weekly menu is a powerful way to stay organized and intentional about your food choices. Start by selecting recipes that align with your goals and include a variety of food groups to ensure balanced nutrition. Choose meals that are easy to prepare, especially on busy days. Consider planning for leftovers; cooking in batches can save time and resources while providing quick, healthy options for the next day.

3. Make a Shopping List

With your menu in hand, create a shopping list of the ingredients needed for your meals. Organizing your list by category (e.g., produce, dairy, grains) can make grocery shopping more efficient. Stick to your list to avoid impulse buys that can lead to unhealthy choices. Additionally, consider shopping at local farmers' markets for fresh, seasonal produce, which can enhance the nutritional quality of your meals.

4. Prep Ingredients Ahead of Time
Set aside a few hours each week for meal prep. Washing, chopping, and storing vegetables can significantly reduce cooking time during the week. You can also prepare grains, proteins, and sauces in advance, portioning them into containers for easy access. For example, cooking a large batch of quinoa can provide a nutritious base for various meals throughout the week.

5. Utilize Batch Cooking
Batch cooking involves preparing large quantities of meals at once, which can be divided into servings for the week. Soups, stews, casseroles, and stir-fries are excellent options for batch cooking. Not only does this approach save time, but it also ensures you have healthy meals readily available, reducing the likelihood of opting for fast food or unhealthy snacks when hunger strikes.

6. Incorporate Flexibility
While having a plan is essential, it's equally important to remain flexible. Life can be unpredictable, and you may find that your original plan needs adjustments. Allow yourself the freedom to switch meals around or substitute ingredients based on what you have on hand or what you're in the mood for. This flexibility helps prevent feelings of restriction and enhances the enjoyment of your meals.

7. Stay Organized
Keep your kitchen organized to make meal prep more efficient. Designate spaces for different types of food and cooking tools. Using clear containers for prepped ingredients and labeled jars for spices can simplify the process of creating meals. An organized kitchen not only makes cooking more enjoyable but also encourages you to stick to your healthy eating habits.

8. Track Your Progress
Consider keeping a food journal to monitor your eating habits and reflect on how your meal planning is working. This practice can help you identify patterns, celebrate successes, and make necessary adjustments. Additionally, tracking your meals can cultivate mindfulness about your food choices and reinforce your commitment to a healthier lifestyle.

In summary, effective meal planning and preparation are vital strategies for achieving consistent healthy eating. By setting clear goals, creating structured menus, prepping ingredients, and staying organized, you can cultivate habits that support your health and well-being. Embrace the journey of meal planning as an opportunity to explore new recipes, enhance your culinary skills, and nourish your body with wholesome foods.

Chapter 3

The Power of Physical Activity

The Benefits of Regular Exercise

Regular exercise is a cornerstone of healthy living, offering a multitude of benefits that extend across physical, mental, and emotional domains. Understanding these advantages can motivate individuals to integrate physical activity into their daily routines, enhancing overall quality of life.

Physical Benefits

The most immediate and observable benefits of regular exercise are physical. Engaging in consistent physical activity contributes to improved cardiovascular health, increased muscle strength, enhanced flexibility, and better endurance. Aerobic exercises such as walking, running, cycling, and swimming strengthen the heart, allowing it to pump blood more efficiently, which reduces the risk of cardiovascular diseases such as hypertension and heart attacks.

Moreover, regular exercise aids in weight management. By burning calories and building muscle, physical activity helps maintain a healthy body weight. This is crucial as obesity is linked to various health issues, including type 2 diabetes, certain cancers, and joint problems. Exercise also plays a significant role in bone health. Weight-bearing activities stimulate bone formation and increase bone density, which is especially important as individuals age and become more susceptible to osteoporosis.

Additionally, exercise improves the body's metabolic functions. It enhances insulin sensitivity, allowing for better blood sugar control, which is vital for preventing and managing diabetes. Furthermore, regular physical activity strengthens the immune system, making the body more resilient to infections.

Mental Benefits

The mental benefits of exercise are profound and far-reaching. Physical activity stimulates the release of endorphins, neurotransmitters that act as natural painkillers and mood elevators. This biochemical process can lead to what is commonly referred to as the "runner's high," a state of euphoria that enhances mood and promotes a sense of well-being.

Exercise is also linked to improved cognitive function. Regular physical activity increases blood flow to the brain, supporting the growth of new brain cells and enhancing overall brain health. This is especially relevant as individuals age; studies suggest that regular exercise can reduce the risk of cognitive decline and diseases such as Alzheimer's. Additionally, engaging in physical activity can improve focus, memory, and learning capabilities, making it easier to tackle daily tasks and challenges.

Moreover, exercise serves as an effective stress reliever. It can reduce levels of stress hormones such as cortisol while simultaneously promoting relaxation, which helps combat anxiety and depression. Regular physical activity fosters a sense of achievement and empowerment, further contributing to a positive mental state.

Emotional Benefits

The emotional benefits of regular exercise are equally significant. Engaging in physical activity can enhance self-esteem and confidence. As individuals see improvements in their physical abilities, appearance, and overall health, they often feel a greater sense of self-worth and accomplishment.

Additionally, exercise can serve as a valuable coping mechanism for dealing with life's challenges. For many, physical activity provides an outlet for frustration and anger, promoting emotional resilience. Participating in group exercises or team sports fosters social connections, which are essential for emotional health. These interactions can alleviate feelings of loneliness and isolation, leading to greater overall happiness.

Lastly, the discipline required to maintain a regular exercise routine can cultivate a sense of purpose and routine in life, providing structure that can be especially beneficial during times of uncertainty or stress.

In conclusion, the benefits of regular exercise are comprehensive, affecting physical health, mental clarity, and emotional stability. By making exercise a priority, individuals can experience improvements in their overall well-being, paving the way for a healthier and more fulfilling life.

Types of Physical Activity

Physical activity is a cornerstone of healthy living, encompassing a variety of movements and exercises that contribute to overall well-being. Engaging in different types of physical activity can enhance physical fitness, support mental health, and improve the quality of life. The four primary types of physical activity are aerobic, strength, flexibility, and balance exercises, each offering unique benefits and serving different purposes in a comprehensive fitness regimen.

1. Aerobic Exercises

Aerobic exercises, also known as cardiovascular exercises, are activities that elevate your heart rate and increase breathing for an extended period. These exercises primarily use large muscle groups and improve the efficiency of the cardiovascular system, promoting better oxygen delivery throughout the body. Common forms of aerobic exercise include:

- **Walking:** An accessible and low-impact option that can be easily incorporated into daily routines.
- **Running or Jogging:** Higher intensity cardiovascular exercises that can significantly boost endurance and stamina.
- **Cycling:** Whether on a stationary bike or out on the road, cycling is an excellent way to improve cardiovascular fitness while being easy on the joints.
- **Swimming:** A full-body workout that enhances cardiorespiratory fitness while providing resistance and reducing the risk of injury.
- **Dancing:** A fun way to engage in aerobic activity that can also improve coordination and boost mood.

Regular participation in aerobic exercises can lower the risk of chronic diseases, such as heart disease, diabetes, and obesity, while also enhancing mood and reducing symptoms of anxiety and depression.

2. Strength Exercises

Strength exercises, or resistance training, focus on building muscle mass, strength, and endurance. This type of physical activity involves working against a force, such as weights, resistance bands, or body weight. Strength training is vital for maintaining muscle mass as we age, improving metabolism, and enhancing bone density. Common strength exercises include:

- **Weightlifting:** Using free weights or machines to target specific muscle groups.
- **Bodyweight Exercises:** Movements such as push-ups, squats, and lunges that utilize one's body weight for resistance.
- **Resistance Band Workouts:** Exercises that incorporate elastic bands to create tension and resistance.

Strength training not only improves physical appearance and functional fitness but also has significant benefits for mental health, enhancing self-esteem and reducing symptoms of anxiety.

3. Flexibility Exercises

Flexibility exercises are designed to improve the range of motion in joints and muscles, enhancing overall mobility and reducing the risk of injury. These exercises are essential for maintaining functional independence, especially as we age. Common flexibility activities include:

- **Stretching:** Static stretches where muscles are elongated and held for a period, and dynamic stretches that involve movement through a range of motion.
- **Yoga:** A holistic practice that combines stretching, strength, and mindfulness, promoting both physical flexibility and mental relaxation.
- **Pilates:** A method focusing on core strength, flexibility, and overall body awareness through controlled movements.

Incorporating flexibility exercises into a fitness routine can improve posture, reduce muscle tension, and enhance athletic performance.

4. Balance Exercises
Balance exercises enhance stability and coordination, which are particularly important for preventing falls, especially in older adults. These exercises engage core muscles and improve proprioception (the body's ability to sense its position). Common balance exercises include:

- **Standing on One Leg:** Simple yet effective for improving stability.
- **Tai Chi:** A gentle form of martial arts that emphasizes slow, controlled movements and balance.
- **Balance Boards:** Equipment designed to challenge stability and engage core muscles.

Regular practice of balance exercises can enhance overall physical performance and reduce the risk of injuries related to falls.

Conclusion
Incorporating a variety of physical activities into your routine is essential for achieving optimal health. Aerobic, strength, flexibility, and balance exercises each play a vital role in supporting physical fitness, enhancing mental well-being, and fostering a balanced lifestyle. By understanding and integrating these types of physical activities, individuals can create a comprehensive fitness plan that meets their unique health needs and goals.

Creating a Fitness Plan
Developing a sustainable fitness plan is essential for maintaining physical health, enhancing mental well-being, and ensuring long-term adherence to an active lifestyle. A well-structured fitness plan not only helps you achieve your health goals but also fits seamlessly into your daily life, thereby increasing the likelihood of consistency. Below are key components and strategies for creating a fitness plan that works for you.

1. Assess Your Current Fitness Level:

Before embarking on a fitness journey, it is crucial to evaluate your current fitness level. Consider factors such as your exercise experience, recent physical activity, and any health conditions that may impact your ability to engage in certain types of exercises. This self-assessment can guide you in setting realistic goals and selecting appropriate activities.

2. Set SMART Goals:

Once you understand your starting point, set specific, measurable, achievable, relevant, and time-bound (SMART) goals. For example, instead of saying, "I want to get fit," specify "I will run for 30 minutes, three times a week, for the next month." SMART goals provide clarity and direction, making it easier to track progress and stay motivated.

3. Determine Your Preferences:

Incorporate activities that you enjoy into your fitness plan. Engaging in exercises you find pleasurable increases the likelihood of sticking with your routine. Consider a variety of activities—such as swimming, cycling, dancing, or group fitness classes—to keep your regimen enjoyable and prevent boredom.

4. Plan Your Weekly Schedule:

Consistency is key to a successful fitness plan. Schedule your workouts at specific times during the week, treating them like important appointments. Aim for a mix of cardiovascular, strength, flexibility, and balance exercises. The American Heart Association recommends at least 150 minutes of moderate-intensity aerobic activity or 75 minutes of vigorous activity each week, coupled with muscle-strengthening exercises on two or more days.

5. Incorporate Variety:

To prevent plateaus and maintain motivation, introduce variety into your workouts. This can involve changing the types of exercises, increasing intensity, or trying new fitness classes. Adding variety not only keeps your routine fresh but also challenges your body in different ways, promoting overall fitness and reducing the risk of injury.

6. Listen to Your Body:

As you progress, it's important to listen to your body and adjust your plan accordingly. If you experience fatigue, pain, or discomfort, consider modifying your activities or incorporating additional rest days. Recognizing when to push yourself and when to take a step back is essential for long-term sustainability.

7. Include Rest and Recovery:
Rest days are crucial for recovery and preventing burnout. Ensure your fitness plan incorporates regular rest days, which allow your muscles to repair and grow stronger. Active recovery, such as light yoga or walking, can also be beneficial on these days.

8. Track Your Progress:
Keeping a record of your workouts, achievements, and feelings about your fitness journey can provide motivation and accountability. Consider using fitness apps, journals, or wearable devices to monitor your progress. Tracking allows you to celebrate small wins and adjust your goals as needed.

9. Stay Flexible:
Life can be unpredictable, and your fitness plan should allow for flexibility. If you miss a workout or face a schedule change, don't be discouraged. Adjust your routine as needed without guilt and focus on staying committed to your overall goals.

10. Seek Support:
Consider enlisting a workout partner, joining a fitness group, or hiring a personal trainer. Having support can enhance motivation, provide accountability, and make exercising more enjoyable.

By following these guidelines, you can create a sustainable fitness plan that not only fits your lifestyle but also promotes lasting health and well-being. Remember, the journey to fitness is personal and should be approached with patience and perseverance. Embrace the process, and enjoy the benefits of a more active life!

Overcoming Exercise Barriers
Engaging in regular physical activity is a cornerstone of a healthy lifestyle, yet many individuals encounter barriers that impede their ability to exercise consistently. Understanding these barriers and implementing effective strategies to overcome them is essential for fostering a sustainable fitness routine. Here, we explore common obstacles to exercise and provide actionable strategies to enhance motivation and consistency.

Identifying Common Barriers
Before tackling exercise barriers, it's crucial to identify what they are. Common barriers include:
1. Time Constraints: Many individuals cite a lack of time as a primary reason for not exercising. Busy schedules, work commitments, and family responsibilities can make it challenging to allocate time for physical activity.

2. Lack of Motivation: The initial enthusiasm for starting a new exercise program can quickly wane, leading to decreased motivation over time. This can stem from unrealistic expectations, boredom with routines, or simply not feeling the immediate benefits of exercise.

3. Intimidation or Insecurity: For beginners, the gym environment can feel intimidating. Concerns about being judged or not knowing how to use equipment can deter individuals from even stepping foot in a gym.

4. Physical Limitations: Chronic pain, injuries, or other health issues can make exercise seem daunting or unachievable.

5. Lack of Support: Exercising alone can be isolating, and without encouragement from others, individuals may struggle to remain committed.

Strategies to Overcome Barriers

1. Time Management: To combat time constraints, prioritize your schedule by integrating shorter, more effective workouts. High-Intensity Interval Training (HIIT) or circuit training can provide substantial benefits in a condensed timeframe. Additionally, consider breaking workouts into smaller segments throughout the day — even 10-minute sessions can accumulate to fulfill exercise needs.

2. Setting Realistic Goals: Start with small, achievable goals that build confidence and provide a sense of accomplishment. For example, instead of setting a target to run a marathon, aim to walk for 10 minutes each day. Gradually increase the intensity and duration as your fitness level improves.

3. Finding Enjoyable Activities: Choose exercises that are enjoyable to you; the likelihood of consistency increases when you look forward to your workouts. Experiment with different activities such as dancing, swimming, hiking, or group classes until you find what resonates with you.

4. Creating a Support System: Share your fitness goals with friends, family, or join a community or fitness group. Having a workout buddy can provide motivation and accountability. Consider online platforms or local clubs that foster a sense of community and shared goals.

5. Overcoming Insecurity: If the gym feels intimidating, consider starting your fitness journey at home or in a less crowded environment. Online workout videos, fitness apps, or small group classes can provide guidance and support without the pressure of a busy gym.

6. Listening to Your Body: If physical limitations are a concern, consult with a healthcare professional or a certified trainer who can help tailor a program that respects your body's needs. Focus on low-impact exercises such as swimming, cycling, or yoga that can enhance fitness without exacerbating existing conditions.

7. Tracking Progress: Keep a record of your workouts and celebrate milestones, no matter how small. Tracking progress can provide a sense of achievement and motivate you to continue. Use fitness trackers or mobile apps to monitor your activities and visualize your improvements.

8. Incorporating Variety: To combat boredom, incorporate a mix of workouts into your routine. Alternate between different types of exercises — aerobic, strength training, flexibility work, and recreational activities — to keep things fresh and engaging.

Conclusion

Overcoming exercise barriers requires a multifaceted approach that focuses on identifying personal challenges and implementing tailored strategies to address them. By fostering a positive mindset, setting realistic goals, and seeking support, individuals can cultivate a consistent and enjoyable fitness routine. Remember, the journey to physical fitness is a personal one, and every small step counts towards a healthier, more active lifestyle.

The Role of Rest and Recovery

In the pursuit of a healthy lifestyle, many individuals often overlook one of the most crucial components of physical fitness: rest and recovery. While regular exercise is vital for maintaining physical health, it is equally important to understand that rest is not a sign of weakness or laziness, but rather an essential part of a balanced fitness regimen. The body requires time to recuperate and adapt to the stresses imposed by physical activity, and neglecting this aspect can lead to a host of negative consequences.

Physiological Benefits of Rest

When we engage in physical activity, especially high-intensity workouts, we subject our muscles, tendons, and ligaments to stress. This stress causes tiny tears in the muscle fibers, which is a natural part of the muscle-building process. However, it is during rest that the body repairs these tears, leading to muscle growth and increased strength. Without adequate rest, this repair process is hindered, resulting in diminished performance, increased fatigue, and a higher risk of injury.

Moreover, rest and recovery play a significant role in the body's hormonal balance. Exercise stimulates the production of various hormones, including cortisol, which is associated with stress. Prolonged physical exertion without sufficient recovery can lead to chronic elevated cortisol levels, which can negatively impact metabolism, immune function, and overall health.

On the other hand, adequate rest allows for the regulation of these hormones, contributing to improved energy levels and enhanced mood.

Mental and Emotional Recovery

Rest is not only essential for physical recuperation but also for mental and emotional well-being. Engaging in regular physical activity can improve mood and decrease symptoms of anxiety and depression. However, constant training without breaks can lead to mental fatigue, burnout, and decreased motivation. Incorporating rest days into a fitness routine can provide a necessary mental reset, allowing individuals to return to their workouts with renewed focus and enthusiasm.

Additionally, rest days offer the opportunity to engage in other forms of self-care, such as mindfulness practices, social interactions, and leisure activities. These activities contribute to emotional resilience and overall life satisfaction, creating a more holistic approach to health and well-being.

Types of Recovery

Recovery can take many forms. Active recovery, which involves low-intensity activities such as walking, yoga, or gentle stretching, can promote blood flow to the muscles without adding significant stress. Passive recovery, on the other hand, involves complete rest and is vital after intense training sessions. Both forms of recovery are essential for different phases of a training cycle.

Sleep is another critical aspect of recovery that is often overlooked. Quality sleep allows the body to undergo essential repair processes and plays a crucial role in cognitive function and emotional regulation. Aim for 7-9 hours of sleep per night to ensure optimal recovery and performance.

Incorporating Rest into Your Routine

To reap the benefits of rest and recovery, it is important to incorporate rest days into your fitness routine intentionally. A general guideline is to allow at least one to two rest days per week, depending on the intensity of your workouts. Listen to your body; if you feel fatigued or notice a decrease in performance, it may be a sign that you need additional recovery time.

In conclusion, rest and recovery are integral components of a healthy lifestyle. By prioritizing these aspects, individuals can enhance their physical performance, promote mental well-being, and ultimately foster a more sustainable approach to fitness. Embracing rest as a vital part of your health journey will not only improve your results but also lead to a more balanced and fulfilling life.

Chapter 4

Mental and Emotional Well-Being

Understanding Mental Health

Mental health is a crucial component of overall well-being, influencing how individuals think, feel, and behave in their daily lives. It encompasses emotional, psychological, and social well-being, significantly affecting how we cope with stress, relate to others, and make choices. Mental health is not merely the absence of mental illness; rather, it is a dynamic state of well-being that enables us to realize our potential, work productively, and contribute to our communities.

The Interconnection of Mental and Physical Health

Research has consistently shown a strong correlation between mental and physical health. Poor mental health can lead to a range of physical health issues, such as chronic conditions (e.g., heart disease, diabetes, obesity) and even accelerate the onset of chronic diseases. Conversely, physical health problems can negatively impact mental well-being, creating a vicious cycle where each aspect exacerbates the other. For instance, individuals suffering from chronic pain may experience depression and anxiety, while those with mental health disorders may neglect their physical health, leading to further complications.

The Influence of Mental Health on Daily Life

Mental health shapes our daily experiences and interactions. It affects our mood, behavior, and cognitive functions, influencing our ability to handle stress and engage with the world around us. Positive mental health can enhance our capacity for resilience, allowing us to navigate life's challenges more effectively. Conversely, poor mental health can lead to difficulties in decision-making, impaired concentration, and reduced productivity. These challenges can manifest in various ways, such as decreased job performance, strained relationships, and diminished quality of life.

Emotional Well-Being and Relationships

Emotional well-being is a key aspect of mental health. It involves the ability to understand and manage one's feelings, leading to healthier relationships. When individuals possess strong emotional intelligence, they can communicate their needs and feelings effectively, fostering deeper connections with others. Healthy relationships, in turn, provide essential emotional support, reducing stress and enhancing resilience. Conversely, poor mental health can lead to isolation, difficulty in maintaining relationships, and increased interpersonal conflicts, further compounding feelings of loneliness and despair.

The Role of Mental Health in Overall Quality of Life

Mental health plays a vital role in defining the quality of life. It influences how we perceive our experiences and interact with our environment. Individuals with good mental health tend to experience greater life satisfaction, improved self-esteem, and a stronger sense of purpose. They are more likely to engage in healthy behaviors, such as regular physical activity and balanced nutrition, which further boosts their overall health.

On the other hand, mental health disorders such as anxiety, depression, and bipolar disorder can significantly impair one's ability to enjoy life. These conditions can lead to feelings of hopelessness, worthlessness, and a lack of motivation, making it challenging to engage in daily activities. This can create a downward spiral where the lack of engagement exacerbates mental health issues, leading to further isolation and distress.

Conclusion

Understanding mental health and its impact on overall well-being is crucial for fostering a balanced and healthy lifestyle. Recognizing the interplay between mental and physical health can empower individuals to take proactive steps in nurturing their mental well-being. This includes seeking support when needed, practicing self-care, engaging in activities that promote emotional resilience, and cultivating strong social connections. Prioritizing mental health not only enhances personal well-being but also contributes to healthier communities, as individuals who feel mentally well are more likely to contribute positively to society. In this way, mental health is not just an individual concern; it is a collective responsibility that impacts everyone.

Managing Stress Effectively

Stress is an inevitable part of life, arising from various sources such as work, relationships, and daily responsibilities. While some stress can be motivating, chronic stress can have detrimental effects on both physical and mental health. Therefore, mastering stress management techniques is essential for maintaining overall well-being. Below are several effective strategies to reduce and manage stress.

1. Mindfulness and Meditation

Mindfulness is the practice of being fully present in the moment, which can significantly reduce stress levels. Techniques such as meditation, deep breathing exercises, and guided imagery help calm the mind and body. Regular practice can enhance your ability to respond to stressors with greater composure and clarity. Start with just a few minutes a day, focusing on your breath or engaging in a guided meditation session. Over time, you can gradually increase the duration and complexity of your practice.

2. Physical Activity
Exercise is a powerful stress reliever. Engaging in physical activity releases endorphins, chemicals in the brain that act as natural painkillers and mood elevators. Whether it's a brisk walk, a vigorous workout, or a calming yoga session, incorporating regular movement into your routine can help alleviate stress and improve your overall mood. Aim for at least 30 minutes of moderate exercise most days of the week. Find an activity you enjoy to make it easier to stick with your routine.

3. Time Management
Effective time management can prevent stress from overwhelming you. Prioritize tasks by creating a to-do list and breaking larger projects into smaller, manageable steps. Use tools like calendars and planners to schedule your activities and set realistic deadlines. Avoid overcommitting by learning to say no when necessary, allowing you to focus on what truly matters and reducing feelings of being overwhelmed.

4. Healthy Lifestyle Choices
Maintaining a balanced diet, getting adequate sleep, and avoiding excessive caffeine and alcohol can significantly impact your stress levels. A well-nourished body is better equipped to handle stress. Incorporate a variety of fruits, vegetables, whole grains, and lean proteins into your diet. Aim for 7-9 hours of quality sleep each night to enhance your mood and cognitive function. Furthermore, reducing caffeine and alcohol can help stabilize your mood and prevent anxiety spikes.

5. Social Support
Building a strong support network is crucial for managing stress. Share your feelings with friends, family, or colleagues who can provide understanding and encouragement. Engaging in social activities, whether in-person or virtually, can help relieve stress and foster a sense of belonging. Sometimes, simply talking about what stresses you can help alleviate the burden and provide fresh perspectives.

6. Relaxation Techniques
Incorporating relaxation techniques into your daily routine can help counteract stress. Techniques such as progressive muscle relaxation, deep breathing, and visualization can effectively reduce tension and promote a sense of calm. Set aside time each day for relaxation,

whether through yoga, tai chi, or simply enjoying a warm bath. These practices can create a buffer against daily stressors.

7. Seek Professional Help

If stress becomes overwhelming and unmanageable, seeking professional help from a therapist or counselor can be beneficial. Cognitive-behavioral therapy (CBT) and other therapeutic approaches can equip you with tools to cope with stress more effectively. Professional guidance can provide tailored strategies that suit your individual needs.

In conclusion, managing stress effectively involves a combination of mindfulness, physical activity, time management, healthy lifestyle choices, social support, relaxation techniques, and, when necessary, professional help. By adopting these approaches, you can cultivate resilience against stress and enhance your overall quality of life. Prioritizing your mental health is not just an obligation; it is a vital component of leading a balanced and healthy life.

The Power of Positive Thinking

Positive thinking is more than just a feel-good mantra; it is a powerful tool that can significantly impact our health and well-being. The concept of positive thinking involves maintaining an optimistic outlook and focusing on the bright side of situations, which can lead to numerous physical, mental, and emotional benefits. Understanding how a positive mindset influences health can inspire individuals to adopt this transformative approach in their daily lives.

1. The Mind-Body Connection

The relationship between our thoughts and physical health is well-documented. Psychological research indicates that a positive attitude can enhance the body's immune response, lower blood pressure, and reduce the risk of chronic diseases. When individuals focus on positive outcomes and maintain an optimistic perspective, they may experience lower levels of stress hormones such as cortisol. Chronic stress is linked to various health issues, including heart disease, diabetes, and obesity. By fostering a positive mindset, individuals can mitigate the detrimental effects of stress, ultimately leading to better health outcomes.

2. Enhanced Mental Health

Positive thinking plays a crucial role in mental health. Those who practice positive thinking are often more resilient in the face of adversity. They tend to view challenges as opportunities for growth rather than insurmountable obstacles. This resilience is associated with lower rates of depression and anxiety. Studies have shown that individuals with a positive outlook are more likely to engage in activities that promote mental wellness, such as exercise, social interaction, and seeking support when needed. Furthermore, an optimistic mindset can enhance overall life satisfaction, leading to improved emotional well-being.

3. Promoting Healthy Behaviors

A positive outlook can also influence lifestyle choices. Individuals who think positively are more likely to engage in healthy behaviors, such as regular exercise, balanced nutrition, and adequate sleep. When people are optimistic about their health, they are more motivated to pursue goals that align with their well-being. For instance, a person who believes in their ability to adopt a healthy diet is more likely to make nutritious food choices and resist temptation. This proactive approach not only contributes to physical health but also reinforces positive thinking, creating a beneficial cycle.

4. Improving Relationships

Positive thinking can improve interpersonal relationships, which are essential for overall well-being. A positive mindset encourages empathy, understanding, and effective communication—all crucial components of healthy relationships. Individuals with an optimistic outlook are more likely to engage in social activities, fostering connections that provide emotional support. These social networks can act as protective factors against stress and loneliness, contributing to improved mental health.

5. Techniques for Cultivating Positive Thinking

Fostering a positive mindset requires intentional effort. Here are some strategies to cultivate positive thinking:

- **Gratitude Journaling:** Regularly writing down things for which you are grateful can shift your focus from negative thoughts to positive experiences.

- **Positive Affirmations:** Reciting affirmations can reinforce positive beliefs about oneself and one's capabilities.

- **Mindfulness and Meditation:** Practicing mindfulness can help individuals become more aware of negative thought patterns and replace them with positive ones.

- **Surrounding Yourself with Positivity:** Engaging with supportive, optimistic individuals can enhance your own outlook on life.

Conclusion

The power of positive thinking is profound, influencing not only mental and emotional well-being but also physical health. By adopting a positive mindset, individuals can improve their resilience, promote healthy behaviors, and enhance their relationships. As we explore the multifaceted aspects of healthy living, it becomes clear that nurturing a positive outlook is a vital component of a holistic approach to health. Encouraging the practice of positive thinking can lead to a healthier, happier life, making it an essential focus for anyone seeking to improve their overall well-being.

Building Emotional Resilience

Emotional resilience is the ability to adapt to stressful situations, bounce back from adversity, and maintain mental well-being in the face of challenges. In a world that is often unpredictable and filled with obstacles, cultivating emotional resilience is essential for navigating life's ups and downs effectively. This section will explore practical strategies to build emotional resilience, enabling individuals to respond to stressors with strength and adaptability.

Understanding Emotional Resilience

At its core, emotional resilience refers to the mental reservoir of coping skills and resources that individuals draw upon when faced with hardship. It involves not only recovering from setbacks but also learning and growing from these experiences. Resilient individuals tend to maintain a positive outlook, manage their emotions effectively, and possess a strong sense of self-efficacy, which fuels their belief in their ability to overcome challenges.

Strategies for Building Emotional Resilience

1. Cultivate a Positive Mindset: A positive mindset is foundational for resilience. This involves recognizing negative thought patterns and consciously reframing them into more constructive perspectives. Techniques such as cognitive restructuring can help individuals challenge self-limiting beliefs and develop a more optimistic outlook. Keeping a gratitude journal, where one regularly notes things they are thankful for, can also foster positivity and enhance overall emotional health.

2. Develop Strong Social Connections: Building a supportive network of friends, family, or colleagues is vital for emotional resilience. Social connections provide emotional support, practical assistance, and a sense of belonging. Engaging with others during tough times can mitigate feelings of isolation and promote a sense of shared experience. It is important to nurture these relationships by being available to others, communicating openly, and showing empathy.

3. Practice Emotional Regulation: Being able to manage emotions effectively is crucial for resilience. Techniques such as mindfulness and meditation can help individuals become more aware of their emotions and learn to respond rather than react impulsively. Deep-breathing exercises, progressive muscle relaxation, and visualization are also effective tools for calming anxiety and promoting emotional stability.

4. Embrace Change and Uncertainty: Resilient individuals often view change as an opportunity for growth rather than a threat. Developing a flexible mindset can help individuals adapt to new circumstances and embrace uncertainty. This may involve setting realistic goals and being willing to adjust them as situations evolve. Learning to accept that change is a natural part of life can alleviate the stress associated with unexpected challenges.

5. Focus on Problem-Solving: Developing strong problem-solving skills is essential for resilience. When faced with adversity, it's beneficial to break down the problem into manageable parts and brainstorm potential solutions. This proactive approach empowers individuals to take control of their circumstances rather than feeling overwhelmed. Emphasizing what can be done, rather than what cannot, fosters a sense of agency and confidence.

6. Prioritize Self-Care: Physical health directly impacts emotional resilience. Regular exercise, a balanced diet, and adequate sleep are crucial for maintaining mental clarity and emotional stability. Engaging in hobbies and activities that bring joy and relaxation also contributes to overall well-being. Self-care routines can serve as a buffer against stress, allowing individuals to recharge and face challenges with renewed strength.

7. Learn from Past Experiences: Reflecting on past hardships and identifying the skills and strategies that aided in overcoming them can bolster resilience. This process reinforces the belief that challenges can be surmountable and encourages individuals to draw upon their experiences when faced with new difficulties.

Conclusion

Building emotional resilience is a dynamic process that requires intention and practice. By cultivating a positive mindset, fostering strong relationships, practicing emotional regulation, embracing change, enhancing problem-solving skills, prioritizing self-care, and learning from past experiences, individuals can develop the resilience needed to navigate life's challenges. Embracing the journey of building emotional resilience not only equips individuals to bounce back from setbacks but also enriches their overall quality of life, enabling them to thrive in both good times and bad.

Mindfulness and Meditation

In today's fast-paced world, the demand for our attention is relentless. As we rush through our daily lives, it often becomes challenging to pause, reflect, and reconnect with ourselves. Mindfulness and meditation emerge as powerful practices that offer a pathway to improved mental and emotional health. These techniques empower individuals to cultivate awareness, foster inner peace, and enhance overall well-being.

Understanding Mindfulness

At its core, mindfulness is the practice of being present and fully engaged with the moment without judgment. It encourages individuals to observe their thoughts, feelings, and sensations as they arise, promoting a deeper understanding of their inner experiences. By focusing on the present, mindfulness helps break the cycle of rumination and worries about the past or future, which can significantly contribute to stress and anxiety.

Benefits of Mindfulness for Mental Health

Research has consistently shown that mindfulness practices can lead to numerous mental health benefits. By enhancing self-awareness, mindfulness encourages individuals to identify stress triggers and emotional responses, leading to more effective coping strategies. Regular mindfulness practice has been linked to reduced symptoms of anxiety and depression, improved emotional regulation, and increased resilience. Moreover, mindfulness fosters a greater sense of connection to oneself and others, enhancing interpersonal relationships and fostering a supportive social network.

Exploring Meditation

Meditation is a technique often intertwined with mindfulness, though it can be practiced independently. It involves focusing the mind and eliminating distractions to achieve a state of mental clarity and emotional calm. There are various forms of meditation, including focused attention, loving-kindness, body scan, and transcendental meditation, each offering unique benefits.

The Emotional Benefits of Meditation

Meditation promotes emotional health by encouraging individuals to observe their thoughts and feelings without attachment or judgment. This practice can help individuals develop a greater sense of compassion and empathy for themselves and others. By fostering a non-judgmental attitude, meditation allows individuals to process emotions more effectively, leading to decreased emotional reactivity and increased emotional intelligence. Additionally, studies have shown that regular meditation practice can lead to structural changes in the brain associated with improved emotional regulation and reduced feelings of stress.

Mindfulness and Meditation Techniques

Incorporating mindfulness and meditation into daily life can be achievable through various techniques, regardless of experience level. Here are a few practical approaches:

1. Mindful Breathing: Focus on your breath by inhaling deeply through your nose and exhaling through your mouth. Notice the sensations of each breath and bring your attention back to your breath whenever your mind wanders.

2. Body Scan: Lie down comfortably and mentally scan your body from head to toe. Notice any areas of tension or discomfort without judgment. This practice can help increase awareness of physical sensations and promote relaxation.

3. Walking Meditation: Engage in a slow, deliberate walk, focusing on the sensations of your feet touching the ground and the rhythm of your breath. This practice combines mindfulness with movement, allowing for a grounding experience.

4. Loving-Kindness Meditation: Cultivate compassion by silently repeating phrases of goodwill towards yourself and others. This practice encourages an open heart and strengthens emotional connections.

Conclusion

Mindfulness and meditation serve as invaluable tools for enhancing mental and emotional health. By cultivating present-moment awareness and fostering a non-judgmental attitude, individuals can navigate the complexities of life with greater ease and resilience. Integrating these practices into daily routines can lead to profound transformations, promoting inner peace, emotional stability, and a deeper connection to oneself and the world. As individuals embrace mindfulness and meditation, they embark on a journey toward holistic well-being, enriching their lives and the lives of those around them.

Chapter 5

The Importance of Sleep

Understanding Sleep Cycles

Sleep is a fundamental component of our overall health and well-being, influencing everything from cognitive function to emotional balance. A key aspect of understanding sleep is recognizing that it consists of distinct stages, each playing a crucial role in the restorative processes that occur during the night. The sleep cycle is typically divided into two main types: Non-Rapid Eye Movement (NREM) sleep and Rapid Eye Movement (REM) sleep, which together form a cyclical pattern throughout the night.

The Stages of Sleep

1. NREM Sleep: This stage is further divided into three phases:
  - **Stage 1 (N1):** This is a light sleep phase, lasting several minutes. It is the transitional stage between wakefulness and sleep. During this phase, the body begins to relax, and brain activity starts to slow down. People can be easily awakened during this stage.
  - **Stage 2 (N2):** This stage constitutes about 50% of total sleep time. Heart rate slows, body temperature drops, and brain waves become slower, interspersed with brief bursts of activity, known as sleep spindles. This phase is critical for memory consolidation and cognitive processing.
  - **Stage 3 (N3):** Also known as deep sleep or slow-wave sleep, this stage is essential for physical recovery. It is characterized by the presence of delta waves in brain activity. During N3, the body repairs tissues, builds bone and muscle, and strengthens the immune system. Deep sleep is vital for feeling refreshed and energized upon waking.

2. REM Sleep: Occurring approximately 90 minutes after falling asleep, REM sleep is marked by rapid eye movement, increased brain activity, and vivid dreaming. It plays a significant role in emotional regulation and memory consolidation. During REM sleep, the brain processes information and integrates new knowledge with existing memories. This stage is crucial for learning and emotional health.

The Importance of Sleep Cycles

The sleep cycle typically lasts about 90 minutes and repeats several times throughout the night. A complete cycle includes progression through the NREM stages before entering REM sleep. Adults generally experience four to six cycles each night. The balance of these stages is vital for overall health, as disruptions can lead to a host of issues.

1. Cognitive Function: Sufficient REM and deep sleep are essential for cognitive processes such as learning, memory, and creative thinking. Lack of quality sleep can impair attention, problem-solving skills, and decision-making abilities.

2. Emotional Health: Sleep plays a crucial role in regulating mood. Disrupted sleep cycles can increase vulnerability to stress, anxiety, and depression. REM sleep, in particular, is linked to emotional processing and coping mechanisms.

3. Physical Health: During deep sleep, the body undergoes critical repair processes, including muscle growth, tissue repair, and hormone regulation. Chronic sleep deprivation can lead to various health issues, including obesity, diabetes, cardiovascular disease, and weakened immunity.

4. Performance and Safety: Insufficient sleep can impair motor skills and reaction times, increasing the risk of accidents and injuries. Quality sleep is essential for athletes and anyone engaged in activities requiring focus and coordination.

Conclusion

Understanding sleep cycles and their impact on health underscores the importance of prioritizing good sleep hygiene. Strategies such as maintaining a regular sleep schedule, creating a comfortable sleep environment, and limiting exposure to screens before bed can enhance the quality of sleep. By appreciating the intricate workings of sleep stages, individuals can take proactive steps to improve their sleep health, leading to better overall well-being. Prioritizing sleep is not just about feeling rested; it is a foundation for a healthy and vibrant life.

The Consequences of Sleep Deprivation

Sleep is a fundamental aspect of human health, yet it is often undervalued in our fast-paced society. The consequences of sleep deprivation can be profound, affecting various facets of life. Understanding both the short-term and long-term effects is crucial for recognizing the importance of adequate rest.

Short-Term Effects

1. Cognitive Impairment: One of the most immediate effects of sleep deprivation is cognitive decline. Lack of sleep can lead to difficulties in concentration, decreased alertness, impaired judgment, and reduced problem-solving skills. Studies have shown that individuals who do not get enough sleep perform worse on tasks that require attention and cognitive flexibility.

2. Emotional Instability: Sleep deprivation can significantly affect mood and emotional regulation. Individuals may experience irritability, increased stress, and heightened emotional responses. This emotional instability can strain relationships and lead to conflicts, further exacerbating stress levels.

3. Physical Symptoms: Short-term sleep deprivation can manifest physically through symptoms such as fatigue, headaches, and a general sense of malaise. The immune system can also be affected, leading to increased susceptibility to illnesses. Research indicates that even one night of poor sleep can impair immune function, making the body less capable of fighting off infections.

4. Risk of Accidents: The impact of sleep deprivation extends to safety. Sleep-deprived individuals are at a higher risk of accidents, particularly when driving or operating machinery. Drowsy driving is a serious public safety concern, with studies estimating that fatigue contributes to a significant percentage of road traffic accidents.

5. Hormonal Imbalances: Sleep plays a crucial role in hormonal regulation. For instance, sleep deprivation can disrupt the balance of hormones that regulate appetite, leading to increased cravings for unhealthy foods and potential weight gain. Ghrelin (the hunger hormone) increases, while leptin (the satiety hormone) decreases, promoting overeating.

Long-Term Effects

1. Chronic Health Conditions: Prolonged sleep deprivation is linked to an array of chronic health issues. Research indicates that individuals who consistently get inadequate sleep are at a higher risk of developing conditions such as obesity, diabetes, cardiovascular disease, and hypertension. The cumulative effect of sleep deprivation disrupts metabolic processes and contributes to the development of these diseases.

2. Mental Health Disorders: There is a strong correlation between sleep deprivation and mental health disorders. Chronic insomnia and sleep deprivation can exacerbate conditions such as anxiety and depression. The lack of restorative sleep can create a vicious cycle, where mental health issues lead to sleep problems, which in turn worsen mental health.

3. Cognitive Decline and Neurodegenerative Diseases: Long-term sleep deprivation has been associated with an increased risk of cognitive decline and neurodegenerative diseases like Alzheimer's. Sleep is critical for memory consolidation and the brain's ability to clear out toxins. Insufficient sleep over time may contribute to the accumulation of beta-amyloid plaques, a hallmark of Alzheimer's disease.

4. Decreased Life Expectancy: Studies have shown that chronic sleep deprivation may be linked to a reduced lifespan. Those who consistently sleep less than the recommended 7-8 hours per night may experience a higher mortality rate compared to those who prioritize sleep.

5. Impaired Immune Function: Over time, inadequate sleep can lead to chronic inflammation and a compromised immune system. This not only increases vulnerability to infections but may also contribute to the progression of various diseases.

In summary, sleep deprivation has significant short-term and long-term consequences that impact cognitive function, emotional stability, physical health, and overall well-being. Acknowledging the importance of sleep and making it a priority can lead to improved health outcomes and a better quality of life. Taking proactive steps to ensure adequate rest is essential for maintaining optimal health and preventing the adverse effects associated with sleep deprivation.

Creating a Sleep-Friendly Environment

Establishing a sleep-friendly environment is essential for promoting restful sleep and enhancing overall health. The space we inhabit plays a critical role in our ability to fall asleep, stay asleep, and wake up rejuvenated. Below are key strategies to create an optimal sleep environment that fosters quality rest.

1. Control Light Exposure

Light is one of the most significant environmental factors influencing sleep. Exposure to natural light during the day helps regulate your circadian rhythm, while artificial light, particularly blue light from screens, can disrupt this cycle and hinder melatonin production. To create a sleep-friendly environment:

- **Limit Blue Light:** Use blue light filters on devices in the evening, or consider using apps that reduce blue light exposure. Ideally, stop using screens at least an hour before bedtime.

- Utilize Blackout Curtains: Install blackout curtains to block out external light sources that may interfere with your sleep. This is particularly important if you live in urban areas with street lights or have early morning sunlight that penetrates your bedroom.

2. Maintain an Optimal Temperature

The temperature of your sleeping environment significantly impacts your ability to fall asleep and stay asleep. The ideal bedroom temperature for sleep is generally between 60°F and 67°F (15°C to 19°C). Here are ways to achieve this:

- Use Fans or Air Conditioning: If you live in a warm climate, consider using a fan or air conditioning to cool down your bedroom. If it's cold outside, a programmable thermostat can help maintain a comfortable temperature.

- Choose Appropriate Bedding: Opt for breathable sheets and blankets made of natural fibers, such as cotton or linen, which help regulate body temperature during sleep.

3. Minimize Noise Disruptions

Noise can be a significant barrier to quality sleep. Sudden noises can cause awakenings, while constant background noise can prevent deep sleep stages. To mitigate noise:

- Soundproof Your Room: Consider using soundproof curtains, carpets, or even acoustic panels to absorb sound. Weather stripping around doors and windows can also help reduce outside noise.

- Use White Noise Machines: If external noise is unavoidable, a white noise machine or a fan can provide a consistent sound that masks disruptive noises and promotes relaxation.

4. Declutter and Organize Your Space

A cluttered bedroom can create a sense of chaos, making it difficult to relax and unwind. A clean and organized space can promote a calming atmosphere conducive to sleep. Here are some tips:

- Keep Surfaces Clear: Reduce clutter on nightstands and other surfaces. Limit items in your bedroom to those that promote relaxation, such as books or calming artwork.

- Designate a Sleep Zone: Reserve your bedroom primarily for sleep and intimacy. Avoid using it for work or stressful activities, which can create mental associations that make it harder to relax.

5. Incorporate Calming Aromas

Scents can have a profound impact on sleep quality. Certain aromas, such as lavender, chamomile, and sandalwood, have been shown to promote relaxation and improve sleep quality. To utilize scent:

- Essential Oils: Use essential oil diffusers or pillow sprays with calming scents to create a soothing atmosphere in your bedroom.

- Scented Candles: Lighting a scented candle before bedtime can help set a relaxing mood—just ensure to extinguish it before sleeping.

6. Invest in Comfortable Bedding

Quality bedding can significantly affect your sleep experience. Consider the following aspects:

- Mattress and Pillows: Invest in a comfortable mattress and pillows that suit your sleeping style. Whether you prefer firm or soft surfaces, ensure your choices support your body and reduce discomfort.

- Bedding Material: Choose bedding made from hypoallergenic materials if you are sensitive to allergens, as this can improve overall sleep quality.

In conclusion, creating a sleep-friendly environment involves a combination of controlling light, temperature, noise, and organization, as well as incorporating calming scents and comfortable bedding. By thoughtfully modifying your sleeping space, you can enhance the quality of your rest and, in turn, support your overall health and well-being.

Establishing a Sleep Routine

Establishing a sleep routine is a fundamental aspect of achieving quality rest and overall well-being. A well-structured sleep routine not only enhances sleep quality but also promotes physical health, mental clarity, and emotional stability. Here are several strategies to help you develop consistent sleep habits.

1. Set a Consistent Sleep Schedule

One of the most effective ways to establish a sleep routine is to go to bed and wake up at the same time every day, even on weekends. This consistency helps regulate your body's internal clock, known as the circadian rhythm, which governs sleep-wake cycles. Aim for 7-9 hours of sleep per night, adjusting your bedtime based on your wake-up time to ensure you get the recommended amount of rest.

2. Create a Pre-Sleep Ritual

A calming pre-sleep ritual signals your body that it's time to wind down. Engage in relaxing activities that help you transition from wakefulness to sleep. This could include reading a book, taking a warm bath, practicing gentle yoga, or meditating. Establishing this routine can help reduce anxiety and stress, making it easier to fall asleep.

3. Optimize Your Sleep Environment
Your sleep environment plays a crucial role in the quality of your rest. Create a sleep-friendly space by ensuring your bedroom is cool, dark, and quiet. Consider using blackout curtains to block out light and earplugs or white noise machines to minimize disruptive sounds. Invest in a comfortable mattress and pillows that suit your sleeping style. A dedicated sleep space free from distractions (like screens and work materials) can greatly enhance sleep quality.

4. Limit Exposure to Screens Before Bed
The blue light emitted by phones, tablets, and computers can interfere with melatonin production, the hormone responsible for regulating sleep. To mitigate this effect, aim to turn off electronic devices at least 30-60 minutes before bedtime. Instead, engage in screen-free activities that promote relaxation, such as journaling or practicing mindfulness.

5. Be Mindful of Food and Drink
What you consume in the hours leading up to bedtime can significantly affect your sleep. Avoid large meals, caffeine, and alcohol close to bedtime, as these can disrupt sleep or make it difficult to fall asleep. Instead, consider a light snack if you're hungry, opting for sleep-promoting foods such as bananas, almonds, or chamomile tea.

6. Incorporate Physical Activity
Regular physical activity can help improve sleep quality and reduce insomnia. Aim for at least 30 minutes of moderate exercise most days of the week. However, try to avoid vigorous workouts close to bedtime, as they may have a stimulating effect. Instead, opt for calming exercises, such as stretching or yoga, in the evening.

7. Listen to Your Body
Pay attention to your body's signals. If you feel sleepy, don't resist the urge to go to bed. Conversely, if you find yourself unable to fall asleep after 20 minutes, get out of bed and engage in a relaxing activity until you feel tired. This approach can prevent frustration and anxiety associated with lying awake in bed.

8. Stay Committed and Patient
Establishing a sleep routine takes time and consistency. Be patient with yourself as you adjust your habits. If you find that sleep issues persist despite your efforts, consider consulting a healthcare professional to rule out underlying sleep disorders.

By incorporating these strategies into your daily life, you can develop a consistent sleep routine that fosters restorative sleep and enhances your overall health and well-being. Prioritizing sleep is a critical step towards leading a healthier, more balanced life.

Addressing Sleep Disorders

Sleep disorders are prevalent yet often underestimated factors impacting overall health and well-being. While occasional sleeplessness can be a normal part of life, persistent sleep issues can signal underlying problems that require attention. Understanding when to seek help for sleep disorders is crucial to maintaining your health and improving your quality of life.

Recognizing Symptoms of Sleep Disorders

The first step in addressing sleep issues is recognizing the symptoms that may indicate a sleep disorder. Common signs include:

1. Difficulty falling asleep or staying asleep: Regularly taking longer than 30 minutes to fall asleep or waking multiple times during the night can indicate insomnia or other sleep disorders.

2. Excessive daytime sleepiness: If you find yourself feeling excessively tired throughout the day, struggling to concentrate, or often needing naps, this could be a sign of obstructive sleep apnea or another sleep-related condition.

3. Loud snoring or gasping for air during sleep: Snoring can be a common issue, but when accompanied by pauses in breathing, it may indicate sleep apnea. This condition can lead to serious complications, including cardiovascular problems.

4. Restless legs syndrome: If you experience uncomfortable sensations in your legs that compel you to move them, particularly at night, you may be suffering from restless legs syndrome, which can significantly disrupt sleep.

5. Nightmares or night sweats: Frequent nightmares or waking up in a sweat can indicate underlying stress or anxiety issues and may contribute to sleep disturbances.

When to Seek Professional Help

Most people experience occasional sleep disturbances, but if these symptoms persist for more than three weeks or significantly impact your daily life, it is crucial to seek help. Here are specific indicators that it may be time to consult a healthcare professional:

1. Chronic symptoms: If you have experienced sleep difficulties, such as insomnia or excessive daytime sleepiness, for several months, it is advisable to consult a sleep specialist.

2. Impact on daily life: If sleep issues start to affect your work performance, relationships, or overall quality of life, it is essential to seek help. Persistent sleep deprivation can lead to difficulties with concentration, mood swings, and decreased productivity.

3. Underlying health conditions: If you have a pre-existing medical condition such as diabetes, hypertension, or depression, and you notice changes in your sleep patterns, it is important to discuss these changes with your healthcare provider. Sleep disorders can exacerbate existing health issues.

4. Behavioral changes: If you or someone close to you notices changes in your behavior, such as increased irritability, mood swings, or anxiety related to sleep, it's time to reach out for support.

The Role of Sleep Studies

When you seek help for sleep issues, a healthcare provider may recommend a sleep study (polysomnography) to monitor your sleep patterns and identify any disorders. This non-invasive test typically takes place in a sleep clinic where various body functions—such as brain activity, eye movement, heart rate, and oxygen levels—are monitored while you sleep.

Treatment Options

Once a sleep disorder is diagnosed, treatment options may include cognitive behavioral therapy for insomnia (CBT-I), lifestyle and behavioral changes, medication, or the use of devices for conditions like sleep apnea. Your treatment plan will be personalized based on the specific nature of your sleep issues and any underlying health conditions.

Conclusion

Addressing sleep disorders is vital for achieving a healthy and balanced life. Recognizing the symptoms and knowing when to seek help can lead to effective treatment and significant improvements in your overall well-being. Don't hesitate to reach out to a healthcare professional if sleep problems persist; your health is worth it. Prioritizing sleep is not just about rest; it's a foundational aspect of your health journey.

Chapter 6

Healthy Relationships

The Impact of Relationships on Health

Human beings are inherently social creatures, and the relationships we cultivate significantly influence our physical, mental, and emotional well-being. Numerous studies have demonstrated that strong social connections contribute to a longer, healthier life, while social isolation can lead to a multitude of health problems.

Physical Health Benefits

Research has shown that individuals with robust social networks tend to have lower rates of chronic illnesses, including heart disease, diabetes, and high blood pressure. The support provided by friends and family can enhance one's immune system, making individuals less susceptible to illnesses. Furthermore, social interactions often encourage healthier behaviors. For instance, individuals are more likely to adhere to exercise regimens and maintain balanced diets when they engage in these activities with others. Whether it's participating in group workouts, cooking healthy meals with family, or simply sharing health-related goals, social connections can foster accountability and motivation.

Mental Health Advantages

The mental health benefits of social connections are profound. Relationships provide emotional support, which can buffer against the stresses of life. When individuals have someone to turn to during challenging times, they are better equipped to cope with stress and adversity. Positive social interactions release oxytocin, often referred to as the "love hormone," which promotes feelings of trust and bonding. This hormonal response reduces anxiety and enhances overall mood. Conversely, loneliness and social isolation can lead to depression, anxiety, and other mental health issues. Studies have indicated that individuals who lack social connections are at a higher risk of experiencing depression and anxiety disorders.

Emotional Well-Being

Healthy relationships also contribute to emotional resilience. Supportive relationships act as a protective factor against life's inevitable challenges, providing a safe space for individuals to express their feelings and receive empathy. When facing difficulties, whether they involve work, family, or personal challenges, having someone to confide in can help individuals process their emotions, gain perspective, and develop coping strategies. Furthermore, positive relationships are characterized by effective communication, trust, and mutual respect, all of which are essential for emotional health.

The Role of Community

Beyond individual relationships, a sense of community is equally vital for health. Being part of a community fosters belongingness, which is essential for psychological well-being. Engaging with community groups, whether through volunteer work, clubs, or social gatherings, provides opportunities for connection and support. Communities can also share resources, offer advice, and create a collective sense of purpose, which can enhance overall well-being. The feeling of belonging reduces feelings of isolation and encourages individuals to engage in healthy behaviors collectively.

The Impact of Negative Relationships

It's important to note that not all relationships are beneficial. Toxic relationships can have detrimental effects on health, leading to increased stress, anxiety, and feelings of inadequacy. Interpersonal conflicts, unhealthy dynamics, and lack of support can exacerbate mental health issues and lead to physical ailments. Therefore, it's crucial to assess the quality of one's relationships and make necessary adjustments to foster healthier connections.

Conclusion

In conclusion, the impact of relationships on health is profound and multifaceted. Strong social connections enhance physical health, improve mental well-being, and foster emotional resilience. Conversely, negative or toxic relationships can have detrimental effects. Therefore, investing time and effort into nurturing positive relationships and fostering a sense of community is essential for achieving and maintaining overall health. Understanding this dynamic allows individuals to prioritize their social connections as a fundamental aspect of their health journey, ultimately leading to enhanced well-being and a more fulfilling life.

Building Strong Relationships

Strong relationships are a cornerstone of a healthy life, significantly impacting our emotional and mental well-being. Building and maintaining these connections requires intentional effort and a commitment to understanding both ourselves and others. Here are several strategies to foster positive relationships in our personal and professional lives.

1. Effective Communication

Communication is the bedrock of any relationship. To cultivate strong connections, it's crucial to practice active listening. This means being fully present in conversations, acknowledging the other person's perspective, and responding thoughtfully. Avoid interrupting or formulating your response while the other person is speaking. Instead, show genuine interest by asking clarifying questions and providing feedback that reflects your understanding. Non-verbal communication, such as body language, eye contact, and facial expressions, also plays a vital role in conveying empathy and engagement.

2. Building Trust
Trust is essential for any strong relationship. To build trust, be reliable and consistent in your actions. Follow through on promises and commitments, and be transparent in your intentions. Admitting mistakes and being open about your feelings also helps in fostering trust. Acknowledge the vulnerabilities both you and the other person may have; it creates a safe space for deeper emotional connections. Remember that trust takes time to develop, so be patient and understanding with yourself and others as you navigate this process.

3. Show Appreciation and Gratitude
Regularly expressing appreciation for the people in your life can significantly strengthen your relationships. Acknowledging the positive attributes and contributions of others not only makes them feel valued but also reinforces the bond you share. Simple gestures like saying "thank you," writing a note of appreciation, or giving compliments can go a long way. When people feel recognized and appreciated, they are more likely to reciprocate these feelings, creating a positive cycle of affection and support.

4. Set Boundaries
Healthy relationships thrive on mutual respect, which includes respecting personal boundaries. Clearly communicate your needs and limits while being receptive to the boundaries of others. This is particularly important in relationships where emotional or physical space is necessary for both parties. Setting boundaries helps prevent misunderstandings and resentment, fostering a sense of safety and respect in your interactions.

5. Resolve Conflicts Constructively
Conflicts are a natural part of any relationship, but how you handle them can strengthen or weaken your connection. Approach disagreements with a mindset of collaboration rather than confrontation. Use "I" statements to express your feelings without placing blame (e.g., "I feel hurt when..."), and focus on finding solutions rather than dwelling on problems. Aim for compromise and mutual understanding, and be willing to forgive and move on from past grievances. Conflict resolution is an opportunity to deepen your relationship and demonstrate commitment to one another.

6. Spend Quality Time Together

Quality time is essential for nurturing relationships. Prioritize shared activities that foster connection, whether it's a weekly dinner, a walk in the park, or engaging in a shared hobby. The key is to be present and engaged during these moments. Make an effort to disconnect from distractions like phones and work, allowing for genuine interaction and bonding.

7. Support Each Other's Growth

Encouraging personal growth is vital in any positive relationship. Show interest in each other's goals and aspirations, and provide support and encouragement. Celebrate achievements, no matter how small, and offer help during challenging times. When both parties feel that their growth is acknowledged and supported, it fosters a deeper emotional connection.

By implementing these strategies, individuals can create and maintain strong, positive relationships that enhance their overall well-being. Remember that every relationship requires effort, understanding, and a willingness to grow together. As you invest in the connections around you, you will likely find that your emotional health and happiness flourish in tandem.

Setting Boundaries

Setting boundaries is a crucial aspect of maintaining mental and emotional health. Boundaries act as personal guidelines that define where one person ends and another begins, outlining what is acceptable behavior from others and what is not. They are essential for nurturing healthy relationships, ensuring personal well-being, and fostering a sense of self-respect. This section will explore the importance of setting boundaries, the different types of boundaries, and practical strategies for establishing and maintaining them.

The Importance of Boundaries

Boundaries are essential for several reasons. They help to create a safe emotional space where individuals can express their thoughts, feelings, and needs without fear of being overwhelmed or invalidated. By clearly defining personal limits, one can prevent feelings of resentment, stress, and burnout that often arise from overextending oneself in relationships or responsibilities. Healthy boundaries promote self-care, allowing individuals to prioritize their own needs and well-being, leading to improved mental health and overall life satisfaction.

Types of Boundaries

Boundaries can be categorized into several types, including:

1. Physical Boundaries: These relate to personal space and physical touch. Respecting physical boundaries means recognizing when someone does not want to be touched or needs personal space.

2. Emotional Boundaries: These involve separating one's feelings and responsibilities from those of others. It's essential to understand that while you can empathize with someone else's feelings, you are not responsible for managing them.

3. Time Boundaries: These dictate how much time you allocate to various commitments, including work, family, and personal time. Establishing time boundaries helps to prevent overwhelm and allows for necessary self-care.

4. Material Boundaries: These pertain to the ownership and sharing of possessions. They help individuals determine what they are comfortable lending or sharing and protect against feelings of exploitation.

5. Intellectual Boundaries: These relate to thoughts and ideas. They allow individuals to express their beliefs and opinions without fear of judgment or conflict.

Practical Strategies for Setting Boundaries

1. Self-Reflection: Understanding your own needs and limits is the first step in setting boundaries. Take time to reflect on what makes you feel comfortable or uncomfortable in various situations. Journaling can be a helpful tool for this process.

2. Communicate Clearly: Once you have a clear understanding of your boundaries, communicate them assertively and clearly to others. Use "I" statements to express your needs, such as "I need some quiet time to recharge" or "I can't help you with that right now."

3. Be Consistent: Consistency is key when enforcing boundaries. If you set a boundary, stick to it. Inconsistency can lead to confusion and may undermine your authority in maintaining those boundaries.

4. Practice Saying No: Learning to say no is a vital skill in boundary setting. It's essential to understand that saying no to someone else's request can be saying yes to your own well-being. Practice saying no in low-stakes situations to build confidence.

5. Manage Reactions: When you set boundaries, be prepared for various reactions. Some people may respect your boundaries, while others may push back. Stay firm and calm, reminding yourself that maintaining your mental health is the priority.

6. Seek Support: If you find it challenging to set or maintain boundaries, consider seeking support from a therapist or counselor. They can provide guidance and strategies tailored to your specific situation.

Conclusion

Setting boundaries is not just about protecting oneself; it is about fostering healthier relationships and creating a more balanced life. By understanding what boundaries are, recognizing their importance, and utilizing practical strategies to establish them, individuals can safeguard their mental and emotional health. Ultimately, healthy boundaries lead to increased self-esteem, reduced stress, and improved overall well-being, enabling individuals to live more fulfilling lives.

Managing Conflict in Relationships

Conflict is a natural and inevitable part of any relationship, whether it be with a partner, family member, friend, or colleague. How we manage these conflicts can significantly influence the quality and longevity of our relationships. Therefore, it is essential to approach disagreements with a mindset focused on resolution rather than escalation. Here are some healthy strategies for managing conflict effectively.

1. Stay Calm and Composed

The first step in resolving a conflict is to remain calm. Emotions can run high during disagreements, but allowing feelings to dictate your responses can lead to hurtful comments or actions that you may later regret. Take a moment to breathe deeply and collect your thoughts before responding. If necessary, agree to take a short break and revisit the discussion when both parties are feeling more composed.

2. Listen Actively

One of the most critical skills in conflict resolution is active listening. This involves fully concentrating on what the other person is saying, rather than merely waiting for your turn to speak. Show genuine interest in their perspective by nodding, maintaining eye contact, and using verbal affirmations like "I understand." By listening actively, you validate their feelings and create an atmosphere of respect, which can help reduce tension.

3. Express Yourself Clearly and Respectfully

When it's your turn to speak, express your feelings and thoughts clearly and respectfully. Use "I" statements to convey your emotions without sounding accusatory. For instance, instead of saying, "You never listen to me," try, "I feel unheard when I share my thoughts." This approach focuses on your feelings rather than placing blame, which can foster a more constructive dialogue.

4. Seek to Understand Before Being Understood

Before attempting to persuade the other person of your viewpoint, make an effort to understand theirs. Ask open-ended questions to clarify their position and show that you value their input. Phrases like "Can you help me understand why you feel that way?" can be effective. This approach not only promotes empathy but also encourages collaboration in finding a resolution.

5. Identify Common Goals

In many conflicts, both parties share common goals, even if their methods of achieving them differ. Identifying these shared objectives can help shift the focus from the disagreement to collective interests. For instance, if a couple is arguing about finances, their common goal might be financial security. By focusing on this shared vision, both individuals can work together to find a solution that aligns with their mutual interests.

6. Brainstorm Solutions Together

Once both parties have expressed their feelings and understand each other's perspectives, it's time to brainstorm solutions. Encourage open dialogue about potential compromises or alternatives. Be willing to consider various options and collaborate on finding a resolution that satisfies both parties. This cooperative approach can strengthen the relationship and promote a sense of teamwork.

7. Agree to Disagree When Necessary

Sometimes, despite best efforts, a consensus may not be reached. It's okay to agree to disagree. Recognize that differing opinions are a natural part of relationships and do not necessarily have to lead to conflict. Respectfully acknowledging each other's viewpoints can help maintain the relationship's integrity, even in the face of disagreement.

8. Follow Up After the Conflict

After resolving a disagreement, it's beneficial to follow up and discuss how both parties felt about the resolution process. This can help reinforce positive communication patterns and address any lingering feelings. By checking in, you demonstrate a commitment to the relationship and an understanding that effective conflict resolution is an ongoing process.

In conclusion, managing conflict in relationships is about fostering open communication, empathy, and respect. By employing these healthy strategies, individuals can navigate disagreements constructively, leading to stronger, more resilient relationships. Remember, conflicts can serve as opportunities for growth, understanding, and deeper connections if handled with care.

The Role of Community in Health

The concept of community encompasses the relationships and networks formed among individuals who share common interests, values, or goals. Being part of a community has profound implications for health and well-being, impacting individuals on multiple levels—physically, mentally, and emotionally. This section delves into the various ways community contributes to enhanced health outcomes, highlighting its significance in fostering a healthier lifestyle.

Social Support and Emotional Well-Being

One of the most significant benefits of being part of a community is the social support it provides. Engaging with others fosters a sense of belonging and connectedness, which is essential for emotional well-being. Studies have shown that individuals with strong social networks experience lower levels of stress and anxiety, as well as reduced risks of depression. When challenges arise, community members can offer emotional support, practical assistance, and a listening ear, all of which contribute to resilience in the face of adversity.

Moreover, the shared experiences within a community can create a sense of collective identity, which can bolster mental health. For example, support groups for individuals facing chronic illnesses or life challenges provide a safe space to share experiences and coping strategies, leading to improved mental health outcomes.

Motivation and Accountability

Being part of a community can significantly enhance motivation towards personal health goals. When individuals engage in activities such as group exercise classes, wellness workshops, or community health fairs, they benefit from the collective energy and encouragement of their peers. This sense of camaraderie can lead to increased commitment to physical activity and healthier lifestyle choices.

Furthermore, accountability plays a crucial role in maintaining healthy behaviors. When individuals are part of a community with shared health goals, they are more likely to stay committed to their objectives. This accountability can manifest in various forms, such as workout buddies, community challenges, or group discussions about nutrition and wellness. The desire to contribute to the group's success often motivates individuals to stay on track, making healthy living a shared endeavor rather than a solitary task.

Access to Resources and Knowledge Sharing

Communities often provide access to resources that may otherwise be unavailable to individuals. This includes educational workshops, health screenings, and nutrition classes that promote informed decision-making about health. Local organizations and community centers frequently host events that empower individuals with knowledge about maintaining a healthy lifestyle, addressing issues such as nutrition, exercise, mental health, and preventive care.

In addition to formal resources, community members can share personal knowledge and experiences, creating a rich tapestry of collective wisdom. This peer-to-peer learning can be especially valuable in navigating health-related challenges, as individuals exchange tips, recommendations, and success stories that can inspire and encourage others.

Building Healthy Environments

Communities also play a critical role in shaping the physical environment that influences health outcomes. Access to parks, recreational facilities, and healthy food options can significantly impact the well-being of community members. Communities that prioritize health create environments conducive to physical activity, such as safe walking paths and bike lanes, as well as initiatives that promote access to fresh produce through farmers' markets and community gardens.

Furthermore, community involvement can lead to advocacy for policies that enhance public health, such as improved healthcare access, nutritional education in schools, and initiatives to reduce environmental hazards. Engaging in community action not only benefits individual health but also fosters a collective commitment to improving the overall well-being of the population.

Conclusion

In summary, the role of community in health is multifaceted and profound. Through social support, shared motivation, resource access, and environmental influence, communities enhance individual and collective well-being. Fostering a sense of belonging and connectedness not only enriches our personal lives but also contributes to a healthier society. Embracing community involvement as part of a holistic approach to health can lead to lasting improvements in both individual and public health outcomes, underscoring the vital importance of community in the journey towards a healthier life.

Chapter 7

Work-Life Balance

The Importance of Balance Between Work and Life

In our fast-paced, achievement-driven society, the concept of work-life balance has grown increasingly critical. It refers to the equilibrium between the demands of one's professional life and personal life, encompassing family, leisure, and self-care. Striking this balance is essential not only for overall well-being but also for maintaining physical, mental, and emotional health.

Understanding Work-Life Imbalance

Work-life imbalance manifests when the demands of work overshadow personal life responsibilities and leisure activities. This imbalance can lead to a range of negative health outcomes, including chronic stress, fatigue, burnout, and even physical ailments. The effects of stress are particularly insidious, as they can exacerbate anxiety and depression, contribute to sleep disorders, and weaken the immune system. As work pressures mount, individuals often find themselves sacrificing personal time, leading to feelings of guilt and inadequacy, further perpetuating a cycle of stress and imbalance.

Physical Health Consequences

The physical implications of work-life imbalance are profound. Extended periods of stress can trigger the body's "fight or flight" response, resulting in increased cortisol levels. Chronic elevations in cortisol can lead to weight gain, particularly around the abdomen, cardiovascular problems, and higher susceptibility to illnesses. Furthermore, when work takes precedence, individuals may neglect exercise, proper nutrition, and adequate sleep, all of which are vital for maintaining health.

A lack of physical activity can contribute to obesity, diabetes, and heart disease, while poor nutrition can lead to deficiencies that affect energy levels and cognitive function. Additionally, sleep deprivation can impair judgment and reduce productivity, creating a vicious cycle where poor health leads to reduced work performance, which in turn adds to stress and imbalance.

Mental and Emotional Health Impact

Mental and emotional health is often the first casualty of work-life imbalance. Prolonged work stress can lead to feelings of overwhelm, anxiety, and depression. Professionals may find themselves feeling trapped in a cycle of work-related responsibilities, leading to a sense of hopelessness and reduced job satisfaction. Over time, this can escalate into burnout, characterized by emotional exhaustion, cynicism, and a sense of reduced accomplishment.

Furthermore, the neglect of personal relationships as work takes precedence can lead to social isolation. Healthy relationships are crucial for emotional support and resilience. When individuals prioritize work over relationships, they miss out on critical social interactions that help alleviate stress and provide a sense of belonging.

Strategies for Achieving Balance

Achieving work-life balance requires intentionality and proactive strategies. Here are several approaches to consider:

1. Set Boundaries: Establish clear boundaries between work and personal life. This includes setting specific work hours and resisting the urge to check emails or take calls outside of those times.

2. Prioritize Self-Care: Make time for activities that promote relaxation and joy, whether that's exercise, hobbies, or spending time with loved ones. Self-care should not be viewed as a luxury but as a necessity for maintaining health.

3. Communicate Needs: Open communication with employers about workload and expectations can lead to a more supportive work environment. Discussing flexible work arrangements or delegating tasks can alleviate pressure.

4. Practice Time Management: Utilize tools and techniques, such as to-do lists and time-blocking, to manage tasks efficiently. Prioritizing tasks can help minimize the feeling of being overwhelmed.

5. Seek Support: Engage with counselors or support groups to address feelings of stress and learn coping strategies.

Conclusion

The importance of maintaining a healthy work-life balance cannot be overstated. Imbalance not only affects individual health but can also impact workplace productivity and morale. By prioritizing balance, individuals can foster a healthier, more fulfilling life that allows them to thrive both personally and professionally. In doing so, they cultivate resilience, enhance their well-being, and create a sustainable approach to living a healthy life.

Strategies for Achieving Balance

Achieving balance in our lives is essential for maintaining overall health and well-being. In our fast-paced world, where multiple responsibilities vie for our attention, the art of managing time and priorities becomes increasingly crucial. Here are some effective strategies to help you cultivate a balanced lifestyle.

1. Prioritize Your Tasks

Understanding what is most important to you is the first step in achieving balance. Begin by identifying your core values and long-term goals. Make a list of tasks and categorize them based on urgency and importance using a matrix. The Eisenhower Box, for example, can help you determine what to tackle immediately, what to schedule for later, what to delegate, and what to drop altogether. This prioritization will make it easier to focus on what truly matters and minimize distractions.

2. Set Realistic Goals

Setting achievable goals is vital to maintaining balance. Break larger objectives into smaller, manageable tasks. Use the SMART criteria—Specific, Measurable, Achievable, Relevant, and Time-bound—to ensure your goals are structured effectively. By doing so, you can track your progress and celebrate small victories along the way, fostering motivation and a sense of accomplishment.

3. Create a Structured Schedule

A structured daily and weekly schedule can help you maintain balance. Allocate specific time blocks for work, exercise, family, leisure, and self-care. Utilize digital tools like calendars or productivity apps to set reminders and keep you accountable. Be mindful to include buffer time for unexpected events or delays, which can help reduce stress and prevent feelings of overwhelm.

4. Establish Boundaries

Setting clear boundaries between work and personal life is essential to achieving balance. Communicate your availability to colleagues and family members, and stick to these limits. For instance, designate specific work hours and resist the temptation to check emails or messages outside of these times. Additionally, learn to say no when commitments threaten to encroach on your time and energy, allowing you to focus on what you value most.

5. Incorporate Self-Care

Self-care is not a luxury; it is a necessity for achieving balance. Make time for activities that rejuvenate your mind, body, and spirit, such as exercise, hobbies, reading, or meditation.

Schedule regular breaks throughout your day to recharge, as this can enhance your productivity and overall well-being. Remember, taking care of yourself enables you to take care of others more effectively.

6. Practice Mindfulness

Mindfulness techniques can significantly enhance your ability to manage time and priorities. By practicing mindfulness, you become more aware of your thoughts, feelings, and surroundings, allowing you to make intentional choices rather than reacting impulsively. Techniques like deep breathing exercises, meditation, or even simple moments of reflection can help center your mind and cultivate a sense of peace amidst the chaos of daily life.

7. Evaluate and Adjust Regularly

Achieving balance is an ongoing process. Regularly evaluate your time management strategies and assess whether they align with your current goals and circumstances. Life is dynamic, and your approach to balance may require adjustments over time. Be flexible and willing to adapt your strategies as necessary, ensuring they continue to serve your well-being.

In conclusion, achieving balance in life requires intentional effort and ongoing adjustments. By prioritizing tasks, setting realistic goals, creating a structured schedule, establishing boundaries, incorporating self-care, practicing mindfulness, and regularly evaluating your strategies, you can manage your time and priorities more effectively. This balanced approach not only enhances your productivity and focus but also nurtures your mental, emotional, and physical well-being, fostering a healthier, more fulfilling life.

Dealing with Burnout

Burnout is a state of emotional, physical, and mental exhaustion caused by prolonged and excessive stress. It often manifests in various spheres of life, including work, relationships, and personal pursuits, leading to feelings of helplessness, cynicism, and inefficacy. Understanding how to recognize the signs of burnout and implement recovery strategies is crucial for maintaining overall well-being.

Recognizing Burnout

The first step in combating burnout is recognizing its signs and symptoms. Common indicators include:

1. Emotional Symptoms: These may manifest as feelings of helplessness, irritability, and emotional detachment from work or personal responsibilities. Individuals may find it increasingly difficult to muster enthusiasm for activities they once enjoyed.

2. Physical Symptoms: Chronic fatigue, insomnia, and frequent headaches or muscle tension are prevalent physical signs of burnout. These symptoms can significantly disrupt daily life and contribute to further stress.

3. Behavioral Changes: Individuals experiencing burnout may exhibit changes in behavior, such as increased absenteeism, reduced productivity, or withdrawal from social interactions. A noticeable decline in performance at work or in personal relationships can also indicate burnout.

4. Cognitive Impairments: Cognitive symptoms may include difficulty concentrating, forgetfulness, and impaired decision-making abilities. These cognitive challenges can worsen feelings of inadequacy and frustration.

Recognizing these symptoms early on is vital for preventing burnout from becoming a chronic condition. Self-awareness plays a significant role in identifying when you might be approaching a breaking point.

Recovering from Burnout
Once burnout is recognized, recovery can begin. Here are several strategies that can help individuals regain their energy and enthusiasm for life:

1. Prioritize Self-Care: Self-care is essential during recovery from burnout. This includes ensuring adequate sleep, maintaining a balanced diet, and engaging in regular physical activity. Activities that promote relaxation, such as yoga, meditation, or simply spending time in nature, can also alleviate stress.

2. Set Boundaries: Learning to say no and setting clear boundaries can help protect your time and energy. Evaluate your commitments and prioritize tasks that align with your values and goals. It may be necessary to delegate responsibilities or reduce obligations that contribute to stress.

3. Seek Support: Connecting with others can provide emotional relief and perspective. Consider talking to friends, family, or a mental health professional about your feelings. Support groups or therapy can also be beneficial, offering a safe space to share experiences and learn coping strategies.

4. Reassess Goals and Values: Take time to reflect on what truly matters to you. Reassessing your goals and aligning them with your core values can reignite your passion and motivation. Engaging in activities that resonate with your interests can foster a sense of fulfillment and purpose.

5. Take Breaks and Vacations: Regular breaks during the workday can prevent burnout from building up. Short, frequent breaks to stretch, walk, or engage in a hobby can rejuvenate the mind. Planning longer vacations or time away from work can provide a necessary reset and allow for deeper relaxation.

6. Practice Mindfulness: Mindfulness practices, such as meditation or deep-breathing exercises, can help ground you in the present moment. These practices can reduce stress, enhance self-awareness, and foster a greater appreciation for daily experiences.

7. Focus on the Positive: Cultivating a positive mindset can shift your perspective. Keep a gratitude journal, noting things you are thankful for daily. Focusing on the positive aspects of your life can help counterbalance feelings of negativity and hopelessness.

In conclusion, recognizing and recovering from burnout is a process that takes time and effort. By implementing strategies that prioritize self-care, set boundaries, seek support, and cultivate mindfulness, individuals can reclaim their energy and enthusiasm for life. Remember, burnout is not a personal failure; it is a signal that change is needed. Embracing this change can lead to a healthier, more balanced life.

The Role of Leisure and Hobbies

In our fast-paced, often overwhelming world, the pursuit of leisure and hobbies may seem like an indulgence rather than a necessity. However, engaging in activities that bring joy and relaxation is not just a pleasant diversion; it is a vital component of a healthy lifestyle. Hobbies and leisure activities play a significant role in improving both physical and mental health, enhancing overall well-being, and offering a necessary balance amid the demands of daily life.

Enhancing Mental Health

Engaging in leisure activities can significantly improve mental health. Activities such as painting, gardening, playing musical instruments, or participating in sports allow individuals to express themselves creatively, which can act as a natural stress reliever. These activities can provide an escape from routine pressures, reducing feelings of anxiety and depression. Research has shown that individuals who regularly engage in hobbies report higher levels of happiness and life satisfaction, as they cultivate a sense of purpose and accomplishment.

Moreover, hobbies often encourage mindfulness, the practice of being present in the moment. Engaging fully in a beloved activity can lead to a state of flow, where one loses track of time and external worries fade away. This state of immersion can enhance emotional resilience, allowing individuals to cope better with stressors outside their leisure activities.

Promoting Physical Health

Physical hobbies, such as hiking, dancing, or team sports, promote cardiovascular health, muscle strength, and flexibility. Regular participation in physical activities not only aids in weight management but also enhances overall physical fitness. Exercise releases endorphins, known as the body's natural mood lifters, which can alleviate symptoms of stress and anxiety.

Furthermore, leisure activities often encourage social interaction, which can enhance physical health through community engagement. Group sports or classes provide opportunities to meet new people, fostering friendships and social networks that encourage a more active lifestyle. These social connections are crucial for maintaining motivation and accountability in physical pursuits.

Building Skills and Confidence

Leisure activities offer opportunities for personal growth and skill development. Whether it's learning a new language, mastering a craft, or participating in team sports, hobbies challenge individuals to step outside their comfort zones. This continuous learning fosters self-esteem and confidence, as individuals take pride in their accomplishments and see their capabilities expand.

Additionally, the skills developed through hobbies can translate into other areas of life, enhancing problem-solving abilities, creativity, and even professional skills. Engaging in diverse activities promotes cognitive function and can help stave off age-related decline in mental acuity.

Achieving Work-Life Balance

Incorporating leisure activities into daily life is essential for achieving a healthy work-life balance. The demands of modern life can easily consume time and energy, leaving little room for personal enjoyment. Prioritizing leisure is an act of self-care that signals to oneself and others that personal well-being is important.

Setting aside time for hobbies can provide a much-needed break from work stress, allowing individuals to recharge and return to their responsibilities with renewed focus and energy. It serves as a reminder that life is not solely about productivity; it is equally about enjoying the journey.

Conclusion

Ultimately, the role of leisure and hobbies in supporting health cannot be overstated. They serve as essential tools for enhancing mental and physical well-being, building social connections, fostering personal growth, and achieving work-life balance. By intentionally incorporating activities that bring joy into daily life, individuals can cultivate a holistic approach to health, leading to a richer, more fulfilling life. As the pursuit of health encompasses not just the absence of disease but the presence of joy and satisfaction, embracing leisure and hobbies becomes not just beneficial, but essential for a healthy lifestyle.

Maintaining Balance During Life Changes

Life is characterized by constant change, be it through personal milestones such as marriage, the birth of a child, career shifts, or the challenges of aging and loss. Each of these transitions can bring about significant emotional and physical stress, making it crucial to maintain balance during these pivotal moments. Achieving equilibrium in times of change involves a combination of self-awareness, proactive strategies, and support systems.

Acknowledge and Accept Change

The first step to maintaining balance during transitions is recognizing and accepting that change is a natural part of life. Embracing the reality that change can lead to growth and new opportunities can help mitigate feelings of anxiety and resistance. This acceptance allows individuals to approach transitions with a more positive mindset, viewing them as opportunities for development rather than as disruptions.

Identify Key Areas of Focus

During significant life changes, it is essential to identify the key areas of your life that require attention. This might include relationships, career, health, and personal goals. By understanding what aspects of your life are most affected, you can prioritize where to allocate your time and energy. Creating a visual or written list can help clarify these areas, allowing you to track your progress as you navigate through the transition.

Establish Routines

Routines provide a sense of structure and predictability, which is particularly beneficial during uncertain times. By maintaining certain daily habits—such as regular exercise, consistent sleep patterns, and dedicated meal times—you create a foundation that can help stabilize your emotional and physical well-being. These routines act as anchors, providing a sense of normalcy even when other aspects of life feel chaotic.

Practice Mindfulness and Stress Management

In times of change, stress levels can fluctuate significantly. Incorporating mindfulness practices, such as meditation, yoga, or deep-breathing exercises, can help center your thoughts and reduce anxiety. Mindfulness encourages you to focus on the present moment, alleviating worries about the future or regrets about the past. Additionally, engaging in stress management techniques, like journaling or talking to a trusted friend, can help process emotions and clarify thoughts during transitions.

Foster Supportive Relationships
Building and maintaining a strong support network is paramount during life changes. Surround yourself with friends, family, and colleagues who can offer emotional support and practical assistance. Open communication about your feelings and experiences can foster connections that help you feel less isolated. Participating in community groups or seeking support from professionals, such as therapists or life coaches, can also provide valuable perspectives and coping strategies.

Set Realistic Goals
When navigating transitions, it's important to set realistic and achievable goals. Whether these goals are related to career aspirations, personal development, or health objectives, breaking them down into smaller, manageable steps can prevent feelings of overwhelm. Celebrate small victories along the way to maintain motivation and reinforce a sense of accomplishment.

Embrace Flexibility
Finally, while it is essential to have plans and routines, embracing flexibility is equally important. Life changes often come with unpredictable elements that may require adjustments to your strategies. Allowing yourself to be adaptable can reduce frustration and enable you to respond effectively to new challenges or opportunities that arise.

Conclusion
Maintaining balance during life changes is a multifaceted endeavor that requires self-awareness, proactive strategies, and the support of others. By acknowledging the change, establishing routines, practicing mindfulness, fostering relationships, setting realistic goals, and embracing flexibility, individuals can navigate transitions with resilience and grace. These practices not only help manage the immediate challenges of change but also contribute to long-term emotional and physical well-being, promoting a holistic approach to healthy living. Through these efforts, you can emerge from life changes stronger, more balanced, and better equipped to face whatever comes next.

Chapter 8

The Role of Preventive Health

Understanding Preventive Health

Preventive health is a proactive approach to maintaining well-being and avoiding disease before it occurs. This paradigm shift in healthcare emphasizes the significance of prevention, which is often encapsulated in the adage, "an ounce of prevention is worth a pound of cure." The concept underlines the importance of taking actionable steps to protect oneself from health issues rather than waiting for symptoms to manifest and seeking treatment. This approach not only leads to improved health outcomes but also enhances the quality of life and reduces healthcare costs.

The Rationale for Preventive Health

Preventive health strategies are grounded in the understanding that many health conditions can be anticipated, and their onset can be delayed or entirely avoided through appropriate measures. Diseases such as diabetes, heart disease, and certain cancers often develop over time due to lifestyle choices, environmental factors, and genetic predispositions. Engaging in preventive health practices can significantly mitigate these risks.

For instance, regular screenings and check-ups can detect potential health issues early on. Conditions like hypertension, high cholesterol, and prediabetes can be identified and managed before they escalate into more severe problems. Early intervention not only increases the chances of successful treatment but also minimizes the need for more invasive procedures or long-term medication, leading to better long-term health outcomes.

Strategies for Preventive Health

1. Regular Health Screenings: Routine screenings are vital for early detection of diseases. Depending on age, gender, and risk factors, individuals should keep up with various screenings, including blood pressure checks, cholesterol levels, mammograms, colonoscopies, and prostate exams. These assessments can help identify issues long before symptoms appear.

2. Vaccinations and Immunizations: Vaccines play a crucial role in preventive health by protecting individuals and communities from infectious diseases. Regular immunization schedules, including flu shots and other vaccinations, help build immunity and prevent outbreaks of preventable illnesses.

3. Lifestyle Modifications: Adopting healthy lifestyle choices is perhaps the most impactful preventive measure. This includes maintaining a balanced diet rich in fruits, vegetables, whole grains, and lean proteins while minimizing processed foods and sugars. Regular physical activity, adequate hydration, and sufficient sleep are equally important. These lifestyle changes can significantly reduce the risk of chronic diseases.

4. Mental Health Awareness: Preventive health is not limited to physical health; mental well-being is equally important. Practices such as stress management, mindfulness, and seeking help when needed can prevent mental health issues from developing or worsening.

5. Personalized Health Plans: Each individual has unique health needs based on genetics, lifestyle, and environmental factors. Developing a personalized health plan that includes tailored preventive measures can enhance one's overall health trajectory.

The Economic Benefits of Preventive Health

Investing in preventive health can also yield substantial economic benefits. By focusing on prevention, healthcare systems can reduce the burden of treating chronic diseases, which often require extensive and expensive interventions. For individuals, preventive measures can lead to fewer medical bills, reduced absenteeism from work, and increased productivity.

Conclusion

In summary, understanding and prioritizing preventive health is essential for fostering a healthier population. The benefits—ranging from early detection of diseases to the economic advantages of reduced healthcare costs—highlight the need for a shift in focus from reactive to proactive healthcare. By embracing preventive measures, individuals can empower themselves to take charge of their health, ultimately leading to a healthier, more fulfilling life. Prevention is not merely a choice; it is a lifestyle that can profoundly impact health and well-being over the long term.

Regular Health Screenings

Regular health screenings are a crucial aspect of preventive health care, allowing individuals to detect potential health issues before they develop into serious conditions. These screenings can lead to early diagnosis, which is often pivotal in successful treatment, reducing the risk of complications, and enhancing overall quality of life. Understanding which screenings are necessary and the appropriate timing for these assessments can greatly empower individuals in their health management.

Age-Specific Screenings

1. Children and Adolescents:

- **Newborn Screening:** Immediately after birth, babies undergo screenings for metabolic and genetic disorders.
- **Lead Screening:** Recommended at ages 1 and 2, and for children at risk until age 6.
- **Vision and Hearing Tests:** Conducted during early childhood and at various school ages to ensure proper development.
- **Body Mass Index (BMI) Measurement:** Starting at age 2, BMI should be measured annually to monitor growth and risk for obesity.

2. Adults:

- **Blood Pressure Screening:** Adults should have their blood pressure checked at least every two years if normal (less than 120/80 mmHg) and annually if elevated.
- **Cholesterol Screening:** Adults aged 20 and older should have their cholesterol levels checked every 4-6 years. Those with risk factors may need more frequent assessments.
- **Diabetes Screening:** Adults aged 45 and older should be screened every 3 years, or earlier for those with risk factors such as obesity or family history.
- **Colorectal Cancer Screening:** Starting at age 45, adults should undergo screening through colonoscopy every ten years or other methods as recommended by their healthcare provider.

3. Women:

- **Mammograms:** Women should begin annual mammograms at age 40, or earlier if there is a family history of breast cancer.
- **Pap Smear and HPV Testing:** Beginning at age 21, women should have Pap smears every three years until age 29, and for those aged 30-65, a Pap and HPV co-test every five years is recommended.
- **Bone Density Test:** Women over 65 or younger women with risk factors should undergo bone density testing to assess osteoporosis risk.

4. Men:

- **Prostate Cancer Screening:** Men should discuss the risks and benefits of prostate cancer screening with their doctor beginning at age 50, or at age 45 if they have risk factors.
- **Testosterone Level Check:** May be considered in middle-aged and older men experiencing symptoms of low testosterone.

5. Older Adults:

- **Vision and Hearing Tests:** Annual screenings become increasingly important as age increases to address common age-related issues.
- **Depression Screening:** Older adults should be screened for depression annually, as mental health can significantly impact overall health.

Other Important Screenings

- **Skin Cancer Screening:** Individuals should conduct self-examinations monthly and see a dermatologist annually, especially those with a family history or high-risk factors.
- **Sexually Transmitted Infection (STI) Testing:** Individuals under 25 or those at risk should be tested annually for STIs.
- **Vaccination Status:** Regular check-ups should include a review of vaccinations, including flu shots and shingles vaccinations, particularly in older adults.

Conclusion

Regular health screenings are essential for early detection and prevention of many health issues. By understanding which screenings are appropriate and when to schedule them, individuals can take proactive steps toward maintaining their health. It is crucial to consult with a healthcare provider to tailor a screening schedule based on personal health history, risk factors, and lifestyle. Prioritizing these preventive measures can lead to a healthier, longer life.

Vaccinations and Immunizations

Vaccinations and immunizations are critical components of public health that serve as one of the most effective ways to prevent infectious diseases. They work by stimulating the body's immune response, preparing it to recognize and combat specific pathogens without causing the disease itself. In this section, we will explore the significance of vaccinations and immunizations, their benefits, and how they contribute to individual and community health.

Understanding Vaccinations and Immunizations

Vaccination involves administering a vaccine, which contains weakened or inactivated parts of a particular organism (antigen) that triggers an immune response. This process leads to the development of immunity, which can prevent future infections. Immunizations refer to the broader process whereby an individual's immune system is fortified against specific diseases through vaccination.

The Importance of Vaccinations

1. Preventing Disease: Vaccinations have played a crucial role in reducing, and in some cases eradicating, infectious diseases. For instance, smallpox was declared eradicated in 1980 due to a successful global vaccination campaign. Other diseases, such as polio and measles, have been significantly reduced in prevalence where vaccination rates are high.

2. Herd Immunity: Vaccination not only protects the individual but also contributes to herd immunity. This occurs when a significant portion of a population becomes immune to a disease, making its spread less likely. Herd immunity is especially vital for protecting vulnerable groups who cannot be vaccinated, such as newborns, the elderly, and individuals with compromised immune systems.

3. Reducing Healthcare Costs: Preventing diseases through vaccination can significantly reduce healthcare costs associated with treating illnesses. This includes direct costs, such as hospitalizations and medications, as well as indirect costs, such as lost productivity due to illness.

4. Global Health Security: Vaccination programs are essential for global health security. Outbreaks of vaccine-preventable diseases can quickly spread across borders, posing risks not only to individual countries but to global populations. Vaccination helps to manage and contain such outbreaks.

Common Vaccinations and Their Benefits
Several vaccines are standard in childhood immunization schedules, including:

- **MMR Vaccine:** Protects against measles, mumps, and rubella. Measles is highly contagious and can lead to severe complications, including pneumonia and encephalitis.

- **DTaP Vaccine:** Protects against diphtheria, tetanus, and pertussis (whooping cough). These diseases can cause severe illness, especially in young children.

- **HPV Vaccine:** Protects against human papillomavirus, which can lead to cervical and other types of cancers. Vaccination is recommended before the onset of sexual activity.

- **Influenza Vaccine:** Annual vaccination against the flu helps prevent seasonal outbreaks and reduces the risk of severe illness.

Addressing Misconceptions

Despite the proven benefits of vaccinations, misconceptions and misinformation continue to persist. Common myths include the belief that vaccines cause autism or that natural immunity is better than vaccine-acquired immunity. Extensive research has debunked these myths, emphasizing that the benefits of vaccination far outweigh any potential risks.

Conclusion

Vaccinations and immunizations are vital for maintaining health, preventing outbreaks of infectious diseases, and promoting community well-being. As part of a comprehensive health plan, individuals should stay informed about the recommended vaccines for their age group and any updates to vaccination guidelines. Engaging with healthcare providers about immunizations can help ensure that individuals and communities remain protected against preventable diseases. By prioritizing vaccinations, we contribute to a healthier future for ourselves and for generations to come.

Preventive Dental Care

Preventive dental care is a critical component of maintaining overall health and well-being. While many people may view oral health as isolated from general health, research increasingly demonstrates the interconnectedness of oral and systemic health. Through preventive measures, individuals can significantly reduce the risk of dental diseases and their associated complications, thereby enhancing their quality of life and overall health.

Understanding the Importance of Oral Health

The mouth serves as a gateway to the body, and the health of your teeth and gums can influence your overall health in various ways. Poor oral health has been linked to several systemic issues, including cardiovascular disease, diabetes, respiratory infections, and complications in pregnancy. For instance, gum disease (periodontitis) has been shown to contribute to inflammation throughout the body, which can exacerbate existing health conditions. Moreover, individuals with diabetes are more susceptible to gum disease, creating a vicious cycle that can complicate management of both conditions.

Regular Dental Check-ups

One of the cornerstones of preventive dental care is regular dental check-ups. These visits allow dental professionals to detect potential issues before they escalate into more serious problems. During these appointments, a dentist will perform a thorough examination, including X-rays if necessary, to identify cavities, gum disease, and other oral health concerns. Early detection of issues can lead to less invasive and less costly treatments, ultimately saving patients time, money, and discomfort.

Professional Cleanings

In addition to examinations, professional dental cleanings are vital to preventive care. During a cleaning, dental hygienists remove plaque and tartar buildup that regular brushing and flossing cannot eliminate. This removal is crucial because plaque harbors bacteria that can lead to cavities and gum disease. By maintaining clean teeth and gums, individuals can significantly decrease their risk of dental issues and associated health complications.

Daily Oral Hygiene Practices

Preventive dental care extends beyond the dental office into daily practices. Brushing teeth at least twice a day with fluoride toothpaste, flossing daily, and using an antibacterial mouthwash can help maintain optimal oral health. These habits prevent plaque buildup, minimize the risk of cavities, and keep gums healthy. Furthermore, a well-balanced diet low in sugar and high in essential nutrients can strengthen teeth and gums, thereby supporting overall oral health.

The Role of Nutrition

Nutrition plays a pivotal role in oral health. Adequate intake of vitamins and minerals, particularly calcium and vitamin D, is crucial for maintaining strong teeth and bones. Additionally, foods rich in antioxidants, such as fruits and vegetables, help combat inflammation and support gum health. Conversely, excessive sugar intake can lead to tooth decay and other oral health problems. Therefore, adopting a nutritious diet not only benefits oral health but also contributes to overall well-being.

Addressing Oral Health Issues

While preventive care is essential, it is equally important to address oral health issues promptly when they arise. Ignoring symptoms such as persistent tooth pain, bleeding gums, or bad breath can lead to more severe health problems. Seeking timely intervention from a dental professional can prevent complications and safeguard both oral and overall health.

Conclusion

In summary, preventive dental care is integral to maintaining overall well-being. Through regular dental check-ups, professional cleanings, diligent personal oral hygiene practices, and a nutritious diet, individuals can protect their oral health and reduce the risk of systemic diseases. By prioritizing oral health, we not only enhance our smiles but also fortify our bodies against a host of health challenges, reinforcing the essential link between oral health and general well-being. Investing in preventive dental care is a proactive step toward a healthier, happier life.

Developing a Personalized Health Plan

Creating a personalized health plan is an essential step towards achieving and maintaining a healthy lifestyle. It involves assessing your unique needs, setting achievable goals, and developing a strategy that incorporates various aspects of health, including nutrition, physical activity, mental well-being, and preventive care. Here's a step-by-step guide on how to design a health plan that is tailored specifically to you.

Step 1: Self-Assessment

The first step in developing a personalized health plan is to conduct a thorough self-assessment. This includes evaluating your current health status, lifestyle habits, and individual preferences. Consider the following questions:

- **What are your current health conditions?** Document any chronic illnesses or conditions that require management.
- **What are your lifestyle habits?** Analyze your diet, exercise routine, sleep patterns, and stress levels.
- **What are your goals?** Identify what you want to achieve, whether it's weight loss, improved fitness, better mental health, or enhanced nutrition.
- **What barriers do you face?** Recognize challenges that may hinder your progress, such as time constraints, lack of resources, or emotional roadblocks.

Use this self-assessment to gain clarity on where you currently stand and where you want to go.

Step 2: Set SMART Goals

Once you've completed your self-assessment, the next step is to set SMART goals: Specific, Measurable, Achievable, Relevant, and Time-bound. For example:

- **Specific:** Instead of saying, "I want to eat healthier," specify, "I want to include two servings of vegetables in my lunch every day."
- **Measurable:** Ensure you can track your progress. For instance, "I will walk 10,000 steps a day."
- Achievable: Set goals that are realistic based on your current lifestyle. Aiming for a daily workout when you currently exercise once a week may be overwhelming.
- **Relevant:** Align goals with your overall health objectives. If improving mental health is a priority, consider adding mindfulness practices to your routine.
- **Time-bound:** Set deadlines for each goal, such as, "I will achieve this within three months."

Step 3: Create Your Action Plan

With your goals in place, it's time to develop an action plan. This plan should outline the specific steps you will take to achieve your goals. Consider the following components:

- **Nutrition:** Plan meals that incorporate balanced macronutrients and micronutrients. Utilize tools like meal planners or apps for tracking your food intake, and consider consulting a nutritionist for personalized advice.
- **Physical Activity:** Develop a weekly exercise schedule that includes a mix of aerobic, strength, flexibility, and balance exercises. Aim for at least 150 minutes of moderate aerobic activity each week.
- **Mental and Emotional Well-Being:** Integrate practices such as mindfulness, meditation, or journaling into your daily routine. Identify activities that promote relaxation and emotional resilience.
- **Preventive Health:** Schedule regular health screenings and check-ups. Stay informed about vaccinations and preventive measures relevant to your age and health status.

Step 4: Monitor Progress and Adjust

As you begin implementing your health plan, it's crucial to monitor your progress regularly. Keep a journal or use apps to track your achievements and setbacks. Reflection is key—evaluate what works and what doesn't, and be open to making adjustments. Goals may need to be modified based on your experiences or changing circumstances.

Step 5: Seek Support

Engaging support from family, friends, or health professionals can enhance your commitment to your health plan. Consider joining a support group, finding an accountability partner, or consulting with a coach or therapist. Sharing your journey can provide encouragement and additional motivation.

Conclusion

Developing a personalized health plan is an empowering process that allows you to take charge of your well-being. By assessing your current habits, setting SMART goals, creating an actionable plan, monitoring your progress, and seeking support, you can tailor a health strategy that fits your unique needs and lifestyle. Remember, your health journey is ongoing, and flexibility in your plan will help you adapt to life's changes while remaining committed to your goals.

Chapter 9

Environmental Factors and Health

The Impact of Your Environment on Health

The environment in which we live plays a pivotal role in shaping our health and overall well-being. This impact spans various dimensions, including physical, social, and psychological factors, all of which intertwine to influence our daily lives and long-term health outcomes.

1. Physical Environment:

The physical environment encompasses our immediate surroundings, including our homes, workplaces, and communities. Factors such as air quality, access to green spaces, and the availability of clean water significantly affect health. Poor air quality, for instance, can lead to respiratory issues, cardiovascular diseases, and other chronic health conditions. Urban environments with high levels of pollution can exacerbate these problems, particularly for vulnerable populations such as children and the elderly.

Access to green spaces is another critical aspect of the physical environment. Research has shown that living near parks and natural areas promotes physical activity, reduces stress, and enhances mental health. Exposure to nature has been linked to lower levels of anxiety and depression, as well as improved mood and cognitive function. Communities that prioritize the development of green spaces can foster a healthier lifestyle among their residents.

2. Social Environment:

The social environment comprises the relationships and social networks that surround us. Strong social connections are fundamental to mental and emotional well-being. Studies have consistently shown that individuals with robust social support systems experience lower levels of stress, reduced risk of chronic diseases, and improved longevity. Conversely, social isolation can have detrimental effects on health, contributing to feelings of loneliness and depression.

Moreover, the social environment can influence health behaviors. Communities that promote healthy lifestyles—such as regular physical activity, nutritious eating, and preventive healthcare—can encourage residents to adopt similar habits. Conversely, environments that normalize unhealthy behaviors (e.g., smoking, excessive alcohol consumption, and sedentary lifestyles) can perpetuate these habits within the population.

3. Built Environment:

The built environment refers to human-made spaces, including buildings, transportation systems, and infrastructure. A well-designed built environment can promote physical activity by providing safe walking paths, bike lanes, and accessible public transportation. In contrast, an environment that lacks infrastructure for active transportation can lead to increased reliance on cars, contributing to sedentary behavior and, ultimately, obesity and related health issues.

Additionally, the design and maintenance of our homes can significantly affect our health. Poor lighting, inadequate ventilation, and exposure to harmful substances (like mold or lead) can lead to various health problems, including allergies, asthma, and other respiratory issues. Creating a safe and healthy home environment is essential for fostering well-being, especially for families with young children or individuals with pre-existing health conditions.

4. Psychological Environment:

The psychological environment encompasses the mental and emotional atmosphere created by our surroundings. Factors such as noise pollution, overcrowding, and the aesthetic quality of our environment can impact stress levels and mental health. High noise levels, for example, have been associated with increased stress and sleep disturbances, while aesthetically pleasing environments (with art, greenery, and clean spaces) can enhance mood and promote relaxation.

5. Conclusion:

Recognizing the profound impact of our environment on health is crucial for creating healthier communities. By fostering environments that promote physical activity, social connections, and mental well-being, we can significantly enhance the quality of life for individuals and communities alike. Public health initiatives, urban planning, and community engagement efforts must prioritize environmental factors to ensure that everyone has the opportunity to thrive in a healthy and supportive environment.

Creating a Healthy Home Environment

Creating a healthy home environment is a fundamental aspect of promoting overall well-being. Our homes are our sanctuaries, where we spend a significant amount of time, and the quality of our surroundings can have a profound impact on our physical and mental health. This section will explore practical tips for transforming your living space into a cleaner and safer environment, ensuring it supports your health and wellness goals.

1. Prioritize Cleanliness

A clean home not only looks inviting but also contributes significantly to health. Regular cleaning can reduce allergens, dust, and pollutants that can exacerbate respiratory issues or allergies. Here are some strategies to maintain cleanliness:

- **Develop a Regular Cleaning Schedule:** Establish a routine for daily, weekly, and monthly cleaning tasks. This can include dusting surfaces, vacuuming carpets, mopping floors, and cleaning bathrooms.

- **Use Natural Cleaning Products:** Many commercial cleaning products contain harsh chemicals that can affect indoor air quality. Opt for natural alternatives like vinegar, baking soda, and essential oils, which can effectively clean without harmful side effects.

- **Declutter Regularly:** Clutter can harbor dust and allergens. Regularly assess your belongings, and donate or discard items you no longer need. This not only creates a cleaner space but can also reduce stress.

2. Enhance Indoor Air Quality

Indoor air quality is often overlooked but is crucial for a healthy home. Poor air quality can lead to various health issues, including headaches, fatigue, and respiratory problems. **Consider these tips to improve air quality:**

- **Ventilation:** Ensure your home is well-ventilated. Open windows to let in fresh air whenever possible, and use exhaust fans in kitchens and bathrooms to eliminate moisture and odors.

- **Houseplants:** Incorporate indoor plants that purify the air, such as spider plants, peace lilies, and snake plants. These plants can absorb toxins and increase oxygen levels, making your home feel fresher.

- **Air Purifiers:** Consider using high-efficiency particulate air (HEPA) purifiers, especially in bedrooms and living areas, to reduce airborne particles, allergens, and pollutants.

3. Reduce Exposure to Toxins

Minimizing exposure to harmful substances is vital for a safe home environment. Here are actionable steps to reduce toxins:

- **Choose Non-Toxic Materials:** When selecting furniture, paints, and flooring, look for products labeled as low in volatile organic compounds (VOCs). These compounds can off-gas harmful chemicals over time.

- **Safe Storage of Chemicals:** If you use cleaning supplies, paints, or other chemicals, store them safely out of reach of children and pets. Consider using childproof containers and keeping them in a locked cabinet.

- Water Quality: Test your tap water for contaminants and consider installing a water filtration system if necessary. This ensures you have access to clean drinking water, which is essential for overall health.

4. Create a Comfortable and Inviting Space

A healthy home environment isn't just about cleanliness and safety; it's also about creating a space that promotes relaxation and well-being. Here's how:

- Natural Light: Maximize natural light by using sheer curtains or blinds that allow sunlight to filter through. Exposure to natural light can improve mood and regulate circadian rhythms.

- Comfortable Furnishings: Invest in ergonomic furniture that supports good posture and comfort. This is particularly important for home offices, where many people spend long hours working.

- Personal Touches: Decorate your space with items that bring you joy, such as photographs, artwork, or mementos. Personalizing your environment can foster a sense of belonging and happiness.

Conclusion

Creating a healthy home environment is a continuous process that requires attention and effort. By prioritizing cleanliness, enhancing indoor air quality, reducing exposure to toxins, and fostering a comfortable atmosphere, you can cultivate a space that promotes physical health and emotional well-being. These small changes can lead to significant improvements in your overall quality of life, making your home a true sanctuary for health and happiness.

Reducing Exposure to Toxins

In contemporary society, individuals are often surrounded by a plethora of substances that can adversely affect health, commonly referred to as toxins. These harmful agents can come from various sources, including the air we breathe, the food we consume, household products, and even personal care items. Understanding how to minimize exposure to these toxins is essential for maintaining optimal health and well-being.

Understanding Toxins

Toxins can be classified into two categories: natural and synthetic. Natural toxins may include substances like mold, pollen, and certain plants, while synthetic toxins are man-made chemicals found in plastics, pesticides, and industrial pollutants. Chronic exposure to these substances can lead to a myriad of health issues, including respiratory problems, hormonal imbalances, and increased risk of chronic diseases.

Strategies for Reducing Exposure

1. Improve Indoor Air Quality

The air inside homes can often be more polluted than outdoor air, primarily due to indoor pollutants like volatile organic compounds (VOCs) emitted from paints, cleaning products, and furniture. **To improve indoor air quality, consider the following strategies:**

- Use natural cleaning products or make your own using ingredients like vinegar and baking soda.
- Regularly ventilate your home by opening windows and using exhaust fans to decrease indoor pollutant levels.
- Incorporate houseplants known for their air-purifying properties, such as spider plants, peace lilies, and snake plants, which can help absorb harmful substances.

2. Choose Natural Personal Care Products

Many conventional personal care products contain harmful chemicals, including parabens, sulfates, and phthalates, which can disrupt hormonal balance and contribute to health issues. To reduce exposure:

- Opt for personal care items labeled as "paraben-free" and "sulfate-free."
- Look for products with natural ingredients and minimal packaging.
- Consider DIY alternatives for items like deodorant, shampoo, and lotion, using simple ingredients such as coconut oil, shea butter, and essential oils.

3. Be Mindful of Food Choices

The food supply can be a significant source of exposure to toxins, including pesticides, heavy metals, and additives. To minimize risks:
- Choose organic produce whenever possible, especially for items known to have high pesticide residues such as strawberries, apples, and spinach.
- Pay attention to seafood sourcing; opt for wild-caught fish to avoid the accumulation of heavy metals such as mercury.
- Read ingredient labels carefully and avoid processed foods containing artificial additives and preservatives.

4. Reduce Plastic Use

Plastics can leach harmful chemicals, especially when exposed to heat or acidic foods. **Strategies to minimize plastic exposure include:**

- Use glass, stainless steel, or ceramic containers for food storage and cooking.

- Avoid microwaving food in plastic containers and opt for microwave-safe glass alternatives instead.
- Choose products packaged in glass or paper rather than plastic when possible.

5. Limit Chemical Exposure in Household Products
Cleaning agents, air fresheners, and other household products can introduce harmful toxins into your living environment. To mitigate this:
- Select eco-friendly cleaning products that are biodegradable and free from harsh chemicals.
- Make use of natural deodorizing methods, such as baking soda or essential oil diffusers, instead of commercial air fresheners.
- Keep household chemicals securely stored away from living areas, especially if children or pets are present.

Conclusion
Reducing exposure to toxins is a vital aspect of promoting health and preventing disease. By making informed choices about the products we use, the food we eat, and the environment we create, we can significantly minimize our exposure to harmful substances. Implementing these strategies not only enhances personal health but also contributes to a healthier planet, fostering a sustainable future for generations to come. Taking these proactive steps can empower individuals to lead healthier lives while cultivating a greater awareness of their impact on both personal and environmental health.

The Role of Nature in Health
In an age dominated by technology and urban living, the benefits of spending time in nature have never been more critical. Research increasingly supports the notion that natural environments contribute significantly to our overall health and well-being. Engaging with nature can provide a multitude of physical, mental, and emotional benefits that enhance our quality of life.

Physical Health Benefits
One of the most immediate benefits of spending time outdoors is the opportunity for physical activity. Nature often serves as a backdrop for activities such as walking, hiking, cycling, and swimming, which can help individuals maintain or improve their physical fitness. Being in natural settings encourages movement, often in an enjoyable and less structured way than traditional gym workouts. For example, hiking a nature trail not only elevates the heart rate but also provides resistance training through varied terrain.

Moreover, exposure to sunlight in natural environments is crucial for the production of vitamin D, which plays a vital role in bone health, immune function, and mood regulation. Engaging with nature can also reduce the risk of chronic conditions such as obesity, heart disease, and diabetes through increased physical activity levels.

Mental Health Benefits
The mental health benefits of spending time outdoors are profound. Nature has a restorative effect, providing a break from the stressors of daily life. Studies show that even short interactions with natural environments can lead to reductions in anxiety, depression, and stress levels. The concept of "nature therapy" or ecotherapy highlights this restorative power, where natural settings are leveraged to improve mental health outcomes.

Natural environments stimulate the senses in unique ways, offering visual beauty, soothing sounds, and fresh air. This sensory engagement can help ground individuals, promoting mindfulness and presence. Simple activities, such as walking through a park, can shift focus away from stressors and reduce rumination, leading to improved mood and increased feelings of well-being.

Emotional and Social Well-Being
Nature also plays a crucial role in emotional health. Being outdoors can foster a sense of connection to something larger than oneself, contributing to feelings of peace and contentment. Engaging in outdoor activities with family and friends can strengthen social bonds, fostering relationships that are essential for emotional resilience. Group activities like team sports or community gardening not only promote physical health but also enhance social interactions, combatting feelings of loneliness and isolation.

Moreover, nature has a unique way of inspiring creativity and problem-solving. Many individuals report clearer thinking and enhanced creativity after spending time outside. This phenomenon is often attributed to the mental clarity that nature provides, allowing individuals to step back from their daily routines and gain fresh perspectives on personal or professional challenges.

Connecting with Nature
To reap the benefits of nature, it is essential to find ways to incorporate it into daily life, regardless of one's living situation. Urban dwellers can seek out local parks, botanical gardens, or green spaces to connect with nature. For those in rural areas, hiking trails, lakes, and forests provide ample opportunities for exploration and relaxation.

Engaging with nature doesn't always require vigorous activity; even simple acts like sitting in a garden, watching the clouds, or listening to birds can be beneficial. Practicing mindfulness in nature—paying attention to the sights, sounds, and sensations—can enhance the health benefits derived from these experiences.

Conclusion

In conclusion, spending time in nature is vital for holistic health. The physical, mental, and emotional benefits of engaging with the natural world underscore the importance of integrating outdoor experiences into our daily lives. As society continues to evolve, prioritizing time in nature can serve as a powerful tool for enhancing well-being, fostering resilience, and nurturing a healthier lifestyle. By making a conscious effort to connect with nature, we can cultivate a deeper appreciation for the environment and improve our overall health in profound ways.

Sustainable Living for Health

Sustainable living is not just a buzzword; it encompasses a holistic approach to living that prioritizes the health of the planet and its inhabitants. Integrating eco-friendly practices into our daily lives can significantly enhance both individual health and environmental sustainability. This symbiotic relationship between personal well-being and ecological health is essential for creating a better future.

Understanding Sustainable Living

Sustainable living involves making choices that reduce our ecological footprint while promoting health and well-being. These choices can range from the food we eat to the products we use and the energy we consume. By adopting practices that are environmentally friendly, we not only contribute to the preservation of natural resources but also improve our overall health.

The Link Between Environmental and Personal Health

1. Air Quality: One of the most immediate ways sustainable living benefits health is through improved air quality. Reducing reliance on fossil fuels by using public transportation, biking, or walking can significantly decrease air pollution. Poor air quality is linked to respiratory diseases, cardiovascular issues, and other health problems. By choosing eco-friendly transportation options, we contribute to cleaner air, benefiting our respiratory health and overall quality of life.

2. Nutrition and Food Choices: Sustainable living often involves a shift towards local, organic, and plant-based diets. Eating locally grown foods reduces the carbon footprint associated with transportation and supports local economies. Organic farming practices typically avoid harmful pesticides and chemicals, leading to healthier food options. Moreover, a plant-based diet is associated with numerous health benefits, including lower risks of chronic illnesses such as diabetes, heart disease, and obesity.

3. Water Conservation: Implementing water-saving practices, such as rainwater harvesting and xeriscaping, not only conserves a vital resource but also promotes the health of aquatic ecosystems. Clean and abundant water is crucial for hydration, sanitation, and agriculture.

Contaminated water sources can lead to a host of health problems, including gastrointestinal illnesses and long-term health issues. By practicing sustainable water usage, we foster a healthier environment and community.

4. Use of Eco-Friendly Products: Choosing eco-friendly household products—such as biodegradable cleaners, natural personal care items, and sustainable materials—can significantly reduce exposure to harmful chemicals. Many conventional products contain toxins that can disrupt hormonal balance and lead to long-term health complications. By selecting non-toxic alternatives, we create a safer home environment that supports physical and mental well-being.

5. Mindfulness and Connection to Nature: Sustainable living encourages a deeper connection to nature, which has been shown to have profound effects on mental health. Spending time outdoors can reduce stress, anxiety, and depression. Engaging in eco-friendly practices, such as gardening, hiking, or participating in community clean-ups, fosters a sense of purpose and community, further enhancing emotional well-being.

6. Community and Social Health: Participating in sustainable practices often involves community engagement and collaboration. Whether it's joining a community garden, participating in local environmental initiatives, or supporting farmers' markets, these activities strengthen social bonds. Strong social connections are crucial for mental health and can provide support systems that improve resilience and overall well-being.

Embracing Sustainable Living

Adopting an eco-friendly lifestyle starts with small, manageable changes. Individuals can begin by assessing their consumption patterns, reducing waste, and prioritizing sustainable options in their daily lives. From composting food scraps to choosing renewable energy sources, every action contributes to a healthier planet and, consequently, a healthier you.

In conclusion, sustainable living is an essential aspect of promoting health. By aligning our personal well-being with environmental stewardship, we can create a healthier future for ourselves and generations to come. Embracing eco-friendly practices not only benefits the planet but also enhances our quality of life through improved physical, mental, and emotional well-being.

Chapter 10

Healthy Aging

Understanding the Aging Process

Aging is a natural and inevitable process that affects every individual. While the journey of aging is unique for everyone, it generally involves a range of physiological, psychological, and social changes. Understanding these changes is crucial for promoting healthy aging and maintaining quality of life.

Physiological Changes

As we age, our bodies undergo a series of physiological transformations. One of the most noticeable changes is the gradual decline in muscle mass and strength, a condition known as sarcopenia. This decline typically begins around the age of 30 and accelerates after 60, leading to increased frailty and a higher risk of falls and injuries. To combat this, regular resistance training and physical activity can help maintain muscle strength and mass.

Bone density also decreases with age, particularly in postmenopausal women, making bones more susceptible to fractures. This process, known as osteoporosis, emphasizes the importance of adequate calcium and vitamin D intake, alongside weight-bearing exercises, to promote bone health.

Metabolism changes significantly as well. Older adults often experience a slower metabolic rate, which can lead to weight gain if dietary habits are not adjusted. Additionally, the body's ability to regulate blood sugar and process fats diminishes, increasing the risk of metabolic disorders like diabetes.

The cardiovascular system also sees changes; arteries may become stiffer, and heart muscles may thicken, which can affect overall heart function. These changes can result in higher blood pressure and an increased risk of heart disease, emphasizing the importance of regular cardiovascular exercise and a heart-healthy diet as one ages.

Cognitive Changes

Cognitive function can also be impacted by aging. While some cognitive decline is a normal part of aging, such as slower processing speeds and minor memory lapses, significant cognitive impairment is not. Conditions like dementia and Alzheimer's disease can occur, but they are not an inevitable part of aging. Engaging in mentally stimulating activities, maintaining social connections, and staying physically active can all contribute to cognitive health.

Emotional and Psychological Changes
Aging can bring emotional and psychological changes as well. Many older adults experience feelings of loss, whether it's the loss of loved ones, independence, or physical abilities. This can lead to increased feelings of loneliness or depression. However, it's crucial to recognize the potential for emotional resilience and growth. Many older adults report high levels of life satisfaction, particularly if they maintain strong social networks and engage in meaningful activities.

Social Changes
Social dynamics often shift with age. Retirement, changes in social status, and the loss of friends or family can lead to feelings of isolation. However, maintaining strong social connections is vital for emotional well-being. Community involvement, volunteering, and maintaining friendships can help mitigate feelings of loneliness and promote a sense of belonging.

Conclusion
Understanding the aging process is fundamental to promoting healthy aging. While physiological, cognitive, emotional, and social changes are a natural part of life, they do not have to diminish quality of life. By adopting a proactive approach to health—through regular exercise, balanced nutrition, mental engagement, and strong social connections—individuals can navigate the aging process with resilience and vitality. Aging is not merely about decline; it can also be a time of reflection, growth, and fulfillment, allowing individuals to embrace new experiences and foster deeper connections.

Nutrition for Healthy Aging
As individuals age, their nutritional needs evolve due to physiological changes that impact metabolism, body composition, and health requirements. Proper nutrition is essential for maintaining health, preventing chronic diseases, and promoting a high quality of life in senior years. Understanding these dietary needs and making necessary adjustments can significantly enhance overall well-being.

1. Changes in Nutritional Requirements
With age, the body's ability to absorb nutrients can decrease, making it essential to focus on nutrient-dense foods. Seniors often experience a reduction in caloric needs because of decreased physical activity and muscle mass. However, their requirements for certain nutrients may increase. For instance, older adults need more calcium and vitamin D to support bone health, as

well as adequate protein to help maintain muscle mass and strength, which can diminish with age.

2. Key Nutrients for Healthy Aging

- Protein: Adequate protein intake is crucial for preserving lean body mass and supporting muscle repair. Older adults should aim for high-quality protein sources such as lean meats, fish, dairy, legumes, and nuts. A daily intake of 1.0 to 1.2 grams of protein per kilogram of body weight is often recommended for older adults.

- Calcium and Vitamin D: These nutrients are vital for maintaining bone density and reducing the risk of fractures. Foods rich in calcium include dairy products, leafy green vegetables, and fortified foods. Vitamin D can be obtained through sunlight exposure and dietary sources like fatty fish, egg yolks, and fortified products. Supplements may be necessary for individuals who are deficient.

- Fiber: A diet high in fiber promotes digestive health and can help prevent constipation, a common issue among older adults. Fiber-rich foods include whole grains, fruits, vegetables, legumes, and nuts. Increasing fiber intake can also support heart health by managing cholesterol levels.

- Healthy Fats: Omega-3 fatty acids, beneficial for heart health and cognitive function, should be included in the diet. Sources include fatty fish (like salmon and sardines), walnuts, flaxseeds, and chia seeds. Reducing saturated fats and trans fats is also crucial for maintaining cardiovascular health.

- Antioxidants: Vitamins C and E, as well as other antioxidants, play a significant role in combating oxidative stress, which can accelerate aging and contribute to chronic diseases. Fruits and vegetables, especially berries, citrus fruits, and leafy greens, are rich sources of these nutrients.

3. Hydration
As people age, the sensation of thirst may diminish, leading to an increased risk of dehydration. Staying hydrated is essential for maintaining cognitive function, regulating body temperature, and ensuring proper digestion. Older adults should aim to drink at least 8 cups of water daily, adjusting for activity levels and environmental conditions.

4. Meal Patterns and Adjustments

Seniors may benefit from smaller, more frequent meals throughout the day rather than three large meals. This approach can help maintain energy levels and improve nutrient absorption. Incorporating a variety of foods into meals can enhance flavor and increase the likelihood of meeting nutritional needs.

Additionally, it is essential to consider any dietary restrictions or chronic conditions that may necessitate specific modifications. For example, individuals with diabetes should monitor carbohydrate intake, while those with hypertension may need to limit sodium.

5. Conclusion

Nutrition for healthy aging is about making informed choices that cater to the changing needs of the body. By focusing on nutrient-dense foods, maintaining hydration, and being mindful of dietary adjustments, older adults can enhance their health, vitality, and quality of life. Consulting with healthcare providers or registered dietitians can further personalize dietary plans to ensure that all nutritional needs are met effectively. Adopting these practices not only supports physical health but also fosters emotional well-being and independence in later years.

Maintaining Physical Activity in Older Age

As we age, maintaining physical activity becomes crucial for preserving quality of life, enhancing mobility, and reducing the risk of chronic diseases. Regular exercise not only helps in maintaining physical fitness but also plays a significant role in mental and emotional well-being. Here, we will explore effective strategies for older adults to stay active and fit as they age.

Understanding the Importance of Physical Activity

The significance of physical activity in older age cannot be overstated. Engaging in regular exercise helps to manage weight, improve cardiovascular health, enhance muscle strength, and boost flexibility. Additionally, it contributes to better joint health, reduces the risk of falls, and can alleviate symptoms of depression and anxiety. According to the Centers for Disease Control and Prevention (CDC), older adults who engage in regular physical activity are less likely to experience chronic diseases such as heart disease, diabetes, and certain cancers.

Types of Exercise for Older Adults

A well-rounded exercise regimen should consist of various types of physical activity to address different aspects of fitness:

1. **Aerobic Exercises:** Activities such as walking, swimming, or cycling improve cardiovascular health and endurance. Aim for at least 150 minutes of moderate-intensity aerobic exercise per week.

2. **Strength Training:** Incorporating resistance exercises using weights, resistance bands, or body weight helps maintain muscle mass and bone density. Aim to engage in strength training exercises at least twice a week.

3. **Flexibility Exercises:** Stretching improves range of motion and prevents stiffness. Incorporate gentle stretching routines or yoga to enhance flexibility.

4. **Balance Exercises:** Activities like tai chi or balance training can help reduce the risk of falls, which is a significant concern for older adults.

Setting Realistic Goals

When it comes to fitness in older age, setting realistic and achievable goals is essential. Start with small, manageable objectives, such as walking for 10 minutes a day and gradually increasing the duration and intensity. The key is to find activities that are enjoyable and sustainable to ensure long-term commitment.

Listening to Your Body

As we age, it's vital to listen to our bodies and be mindful of any discomfort or pain. If something feels wrong, it's advisable to stop and consult a healthcare professional. Gentle exercises, such as water aerobics or chair yoga, can be excellent alternatives for those with joint pain or mobility issues.

Finding Support and Community

Engaging in physical activities with others can significantly enhance motivation and enjoyment. Joining community groups, classes, or fitness programs tailored for seniors can provide social interaction and encouragement. Many communities offer programs specifically designed for older adults, making exercising a fun and social event.

Incorporating Activity into Daily Life

Staying active doesn't always require structured workouts. Incorporating movement into daily routines can be just as effective. Simple activities such as gardening, taking the stairs, or walking the dog can contribute to an active lifestyle. Aim to stand and move around every hour, especially if you spend a lot of time sitting.

The Role of Technology

Technology can play a significant role in maintaining physical activity in older age. Fitness trackers and mobile apps can help monitor activity levels, set reminders to move, and provide guidance on exercises. Online classes and virtual fitness communities can also offer support and motivation.

Conclusion

Maintaining physical activity as we age is essential for sustaining health, independence, and overall well-being. By understanding the importance of exercise, setting realistic goals, listening to our bodies, and incorporating movement into daily life, older adults can enjoy a fulfilling and active lifestyle. With the right mindset and resources, staying fit in older age is not only possible but can also be an enriching and enjoyable journey.

Mental Health and Aging

As individuals age, the relationship between mental health and aging becomes increasingly important, influencing not only cognitive function but also emotional well-being. Mental health in older adults is a multifaceted issue that requires a comprehensive understanding of the various factors that can impact cognitive health and emotional resilience.

Cognitive Health

Cognitive health refers to the ability to think clearly, learn, remember, and make sound decisions. It is crucial for maintaining independence and quality of life as one ages. Cognitive decline can manifest in various ways, including memory loss, difficulty concentrating, and impaired judgment. While some cognitive decline is a normal part of aging, severe cognitive impairment, such as dementia or Alzheimer's disease, is not. These conditions can significantly impact not just the individual but also their families and caregivers.

Maintaining cognitive health involves several strategies:

1. Engagement in Mental Activities: Regularly challenging the brain through puzzles, reading, learning new skills, or engaging in social discussions can help keep cognitive functions sharp. Research shows that lifelong learning and mental stimulation can create cognitive reserves that may delay the onset of dementia.

2. Physical Activity: Exercise is not just beneficial for physical health; it also plays a crucial role in cognitive well-being. Studies indicate that regular physical activity increases blood flow to the brain, which can enhance brain health, improve mood, and reduce feelings of anxiety and depression.

3. Healthy Nutrition: A balanced diet rich in fruits, vegetables, whole grains, lean proteins, and healthy fats supports both physical and cognitive health. Nutrients such as omega-3 fatty acids, antioxidants, and vitamins like B12 and D are essential for brain function.

4. Social Connections: Social engagement is vital for cognitive health. Maintaining relationships with family and friends can provide emotional support and mental stimulation, reducing feelings of loneliness and isolation that can negatively impact cognitive function.

Emotional Well-Being

Emotional well-being encompasses the ability to manage stress, cope with life's challenges, and maintain a positive outlook. For older adults, emotional health can be influenced by factors such as retirement, loss of loved ones, reduced physical capabilities, and chronic health conditions. These changes can lead to feelings of sadness, anxiety, or even depression.

To foster emotional well-being, older adults can adopt several practices:

1. Mindfulness and Meditation: Mindfulness practices can help individuals focus on the present moment and cultivate a positive mindset. Mindfulness meditation has been shown to reduce stress, improve emotional regulation, and enhance overall well-being.

2. Building Resilience: Resilience—the ability to bounce back from adversity—is crucial for emotional health in later life. Developing coping skills, maintaining a sense of purpose, and having a supportive social network can enhance resilience.

3. Seeking Professional Help: Older adults should not hesitate to seek help from mental health professionals if they are experiencing prolonged feelings of sadness or anxiety. Therapy and counseling can provide valuable strategies for managing mental health challenges.

4. Participating in Community Activities: Engaging in community service or group activities can create a sense of belonging and purpose, which is essential for emotional health. Volunteering not only benefits others but also enhances the volunteer's own well-being.

In conclusion, mental health and aging are interconnected aspects of overall health that deserve attention and care. By prioritizing cognitive health through mental engagement, physical activity, and social connections, as well as nurturing emotional well-being through mindfulness, resilience-building, and community involvement, older adults can navigate the complexities of aging while maintaining a fulfilling and healthy life. Emphasizing these aspects can lead to a more vibrant, connected, and meaningful experience in later years, ultimately enhancing the quality of life and promoting longevity.

Social Connections in Later Life

As individuals age, the significance of social connections becomes increasingly paramount for maintaining overall well-being. Studies have consistently shown that strong social ties contribute to a healthier, happier, and longer life. In later years, social connections not only provide emotional support but also play a crucial role in mental and physical health, enhancing the quality of life for seniors.

Emotional Benefits

Social interactions are vital for emotional health. As people age, they may experience losses—be it the death of loved ones, retirement, or the physical decline that can come with aging. These changes can lead to feelings of loneliness and isolation, which are risk factors for depression and anxiety. Maintaining social connections helps mitigate these feelings. Engaging with friends, family, and community members fosters a sense of belonging and purpose. Regular interactions can uplift mood, instill a sense of happiness, and provide a buffer against the emotional challenges of aging.

Cognitive Health

Social engagement is also linked to cognitive health. Research indicates that staying socially active can reduce the risk of cognitive decline and dementia. Conversations stimulate the brain, promoting mental agility and memory retention. Activities such as participating in community groups, book clubs, or simply engaging in meaningful conversations with others can keep the mind sharp. Furthermore, learning new skills or hobbies in a social setting can provide cognitive challenges that are beneficial for brain health.

Physical Health

The impact of social connections extends to physical health as well. Seniors with strong social networks tend to have better physical health outcomes. They may engage in more physical activity, as social gatherings often involve walking, dancing, or participating in group sports. Social support can also influence health behaviors; individuals are more likely to adhere to medical advice, attend regular check-ups, and maintain a healthier lifestyle when they have encouragement from peers and family.

Conversely, loneliness has been linked to various health issues, including increased risk of heart disease, high blood pressure, and a weakened immune system. The physiological effects of loneliness can mimic those of chronic stress, negatively affecting health over time. Therefore, fostering social connections is not only beneficial but essential for sustaining physical health in later life.

Building and Maintaining Connections

To cultivate strong social ties as one ages, it is crucial to actively seek out opportunities for connection. This can include joining clubs, participating in community service, volunteering, or attending local events. Technology also offers avenues for connection; video calls, social media, and online forums can bridge distances and facilitate relationships. For those who may have mobility issues, local organizations often provide transportation services to help seniors attend social activities.

Moreover, nurturing existing relationships is just as important as forming new ones. Regularly reaching out to family and friends, participating in shared activities, and expressing appreciation for loved ones can strengthen these bonds. It is essential to be proactive in maintaining these connections, as relationships can fade without effort, especially in later life.

Conclusion

In conclusion, social connections are integral to the health and happiness of older adults. Fostering these relationships can enhance emotional resilience, bolster cognitive function, and improve physical health. By remaining socially active and engaged, seniors can create a fulfilling lifestyle that enriches their later years, ultimately leading to a more vibrant and meaningful life. Therefore, as individuals age, it is crucial to prioritize social connections and find ways to stay connected to both existing and new relationships.

Chapter 11

The Role of Technology in Health

Health Technology Overview

In today's fast-paced world, technology has become an integral part of nearly every facet of our lives, and health care is no exception. The intersection of technology and health has ushered in a new era of personalized medicine, improved patient outcomes, and enhanced accessibility to health care services. This transformation can be observed through various innovations that are reshaping how individuals manage their health and navigate the health care system.

Telemedicine: Bridging Distance Gaps

Telemedicine has emerged as a revolutionary tool, especially highlighted during the COVID-19 pandemic. With the ability to consult with healthcare providers via video calls or messaging apps, patients can receive care from the comfort of their homes. This is particularly beneficial for individuals in remote areas or those with mobility issues. Telemedicine not only saves time and reduces travel costs but also enables quick access to specialists who may not be locally available. Furthermore, it encourages ongoing communication between patients and providers, fostering a collaborative approach to health management.

Wearable Technology: Monitoring Health in Real-Time

Wearable devices, such as fitness trackers, smartwatches, and health monitors, are increasingly popular for personal health management. These devices track various metrics, including heart rate, physical activity, sleep patterns, and even blood glucose levels. By providing real-time data, wearables empower individuals to take charge of their health. Users can set fitness goals, monitor their progress, and receive notifications that prompt them to stay active or take a moment to relax. This immediate feedback loop encourages lifestyle changes that can lead to improved physical health, making it easier to adopt and maintain healthy habits.

Mobile Health Apps: Personal Health Management at Your Fingertips

Mobile health applications have proliferated, offering tools for everything from tracking nutrition and exercise to managing chronic conditions. These apps often include features such as medication reminders, symptom checkers, and educational resources. For example, diabetic patients can use apps to log their blood sugar levels and receive dietary recommendations tailored to their needs. Such personalized approaches promote better self-management and adherence to treatment plans, ultimately improving health outcomes.

Health Data Analytics: Informing Better Care Decisions

Big data analytics is transforming how health care providers approach patient care. By analyzing large sets of health data, providers can identify patterns and trends that inform clinical decisions. Predictive analytics can help anticipate health risks, allowing for proactive interventions before problems escalate. For instance, hospitals can analyze readmission rates to identify at-risk patients and implement targeted follow-up care. This data-driven approach enhances the quality of care and optimizes resource allocation in healthcare settings.

Electronic Health Records (EHRs): Streamlining Patient Information

The transition from paper records to electronic health records has been a significant advancement in healthcare technology. EHRs centralize patient information, making it easily accessible to authorized healthcare providers. This continuity of care enhances communication among specialists and primary care providers, reducing the likelihood of errors and duplicative tests. Patients also benefit from having their health information in one location, which simplifies the process of sharing medical history during visits.

Future Trends in Health Technology

As technology continues to evolve, the future of health care holds exciting possibilities. Innovations such as artificial intelligence (AI), machine learning, and virtual reality are poised to further enhance patient care. AI algorithms can assist in diagnosing diseases and personalizing treatment plans, while virtual reality can be used in therapeutic settings, such as pain management or rehabilitation.

In conclusion, the integration of technology in health care and personal health management is not merely a trend but a fundamental shift that enhances the way we approach health. With ongoing advancements, individuals are empowered to take control of their health, engage actively with healthcare providers, and ultimately foster a healthier society. Embracing these technologies can lead to improved health outcomes, increased accessibility, and a more holistic approach to well-being.

Fitness Trackers and Apps

In an era where technology has permeated nearly every aspect of our lives, fitness tracking devices and applications are revolutionizing the way we approach physical activity and health management. These tools not only help individuals monitor their fitness levels but also provide insights and motivation that can lead to improved health outcomes. Understanding how to effectively use fitness trackers and apps can empower individuals to take control of their fitness journeys.

Understanding Fitness Trackers

Fitness trackers come in various forms, from simple pedometers that count steps to advanced smartwatches that monitor heart rate, sleep patterns, and even stress levels. These devices utilize sensors and algorithms to provide users with real-time data about their physical activities. By wearing a fitness tracker, users can easily track metrics such as steps taken, calories burned, distance traveled, and active minutes throughout the day.

Choosing the Right Fitness Tracker

When selecting a fitness tracker, it's essential to consider personal goals and preferences. Some key factors to think about include:

1. Features: Determine which features are most important. If you're focused on cardiovascular fitness, a tracker with heart rate monitoring and GPS capabilities may be ideal. For those interested in strength training, look for devices that can log workouts and track specific exercises.

2. Compatibility: Ensure the tracker is compatible with your smartphone or other devices. Many fitness trackers sync with mobile apps, enhancing the user experience by allowing for more detailed analysis and tracking.

3. Design and Comfort: Since fitness trackers are typically worn all day, choose a design that feels comfortable and suits your style. Consider battery life as well, as longer-lasting devices reduce the frequency of charging.

Utilizing Fitness Apps

Fitness apps complement wearable technology by offering comprehensive platforms for tracking and improving fitness. These apps often allow users to log workouts, set goals, and monitor progress over time. Popular fitness apps, such as MyFitnessPal, Strava, and Fitbit, provide features such as:

- Goal Setting: Users can set specific, measurable, achievable, relevant, and time-bound (SMART) goals. Whether it's running a certain distance, losing weight, or increasing strength, apps facilitate goal tracking.

- Activity Logging: Many apps allow users to log a variety of activities, from running and cycling to weight lifting and yoga. This feature helps users understand their workout patterns and adjust them based on their goals.

- Nutrition Tracking: Some fitness apps provide nutritional insights, allowing users to track their food intake alongside their workouts. This holistic approach can be beneficial for achieving weight-related goals or ensuring adequate nutrient intake.

- Social Features: Engaging with friends or joining fitness communities can provide motivation and accountability. Many apps have social features that allow users to share achievements, participate in challenges, and support each other in their fitness journeys.

Maximizing the Benefits

To make the most of fitness trackers and apps, consider the following strategies:

- Consistency: Regularly wear your fitness tracker and log activities in your app. Consistency is crucial for obtaining an accurate picture of your physical activity levels and progress.

- Review Data: Take time to review the data collected by your fitness tracker and app. Analyze trends over weeks or months to understand your habits and identify areas for improvement.

- Adapt and Evolve: Use the insights gained from your data to adapt your fitness routine. If you notice that certain activities yield better results or that you're consistently missing your goals, adjust your plan accordingly.

- Stay Engaged: Explore new features or challenges within your app. Many platforms regularly update with new functionalities that can keep your fitness journey fresh and exciting.

In summary, fitness trackers and apps are powerful tools that can significantly enhance your fitness journey. By leveraging technology to track and improve fitness, you can gain valuable insights, stay motivated, and ultimately lead a healthier life. Whether you're a seasoned athlete or a beginner, integrating these technologies into your routine can provide the support needed to achieve your fitness goals.

Telemedicine and Online Health Resources

The advent of technology has revolutionized the way we access healthcare, making it more convenient and efficient than ever before. Telemedicine, in particular, has emerged as a critical component of modern healthcare delivery, allowing patients to consult healthcare professionals remotely, thus breaking geographical barriers and reducing the time and costs associated with traditional healthcare settings.

What is Telemedicine?

Telemedicine refers to the use of digital communication tools to provide health care services remotely. This encompasses a wide range of services, from virtual consultations via video calls to remote monitoring of patients' health conditions through wearable devices and mobile applications. Telemedicine can be particularly beneficial for individuals living in rural areas with limited access to healthcare facilities, as well as those with mobility issues or chronic conditions that make travel difficult.

Benefits of Telemedicine

1. Accessibility: One of the most significant advantages of telemedicine is its ability to enhance access to healthcare services. Patients can connect with specialists who may not be available in their local area, reducing the need for travel and wait times.

2. Convenience: Telemedicine appointments can often be scheduled more flexibly than traditional in-person visits. Patients can attend consultations from the comfort of their own homes, which is particularly useful for busy individuals and families.

3. Cost-Effectiveness: By eliminating travel expenses and reducing the time off work needed for appointments, telemedicine can be a more cost-effective option for many patients. Some insurance plans also cover telehealth services, further decreasing financial barriers.

4. Continuity of Care: Telemedicine facilitates ongoing communication between patients and healthcare providers, making it easier to manage chronic conditions and follow up on treatment plans without the need for frequent in-person visits.

Accessing Telemedicine Services

To access telemedicine services, patients typically need to follow a few simple steps:

1. Choose a Provider: Many healthcare providers now offer telemedicine options. Patients can check their primary care physician's office or look for telehealth platforms that connect them with licensed healthcare professionals.

2. Create an Account: Most telehealth services require patients to create an online account, where they can provide personal information, medical history, and payment details.

3. Schedule an Appointment: Patients can usually book an appointment directly through the provider's website or app. Some services may offer same-day appointments, while others may require patients to schedule in advance.

4. Prepare for the Appointment: Before the virtual consultation, patients should ensure they have a stable internet connection, a quiet and private space for the appointment, and any necessary medical records or questions prepared.

5. Consultation: During the appointment, patients can discuss their health concerns with the provider, who may provide diagnoses, treatment recommendations, or prescriptions as needed.

Online Health Resources

In addition to telemedicine, the internet provides a wealth of health information and resources. Patients can access reputable websites, such as those from government health agencies, medical organizations, and academic institutions, to learn about medical conditions, treatments, and preventive measures. Online resources can empower patients to take an active role in their health management.

However, it is essential to approach online health information with caution. Patients should critically evaluate the sources of information, ensuring they are credible and evidence-based. Misinformation can lead to confusion and potentially harmful decisions regarding health.

Conclusion

Telemedicine and online health resources represent a significant advancement in healthcare accessibility and patient empowerment. By leveraging technology, individuals can more easily obtain the care and information they need to maintain their health and well-being. As telemedicine continues to evolve, it promises to enhance the healthcare experience, making it more inclusive and responsive to the needs of diverse populations.

The Impact of Screen Time on Health

In today's digital age, screens are ubiquitous—found in our homes, workplaces, and pockets. From smartphones and tablets to computers and televisions, screen time has become an integral part of daily life. While technology offers numerous benefits, excessive screen time can have significant drawbacks, affecting physical, mental, and emotional health. Understanding these impacts is essential for balancing technology use with healthy living.

Benefits of Screen Time

1. Access to Information: One of the most significant advantages of screen time is the vast amount of information available at our fingertips. Online resources enable individuals to access educational content, health information, and support resources that can enhance their knowledge and decision-making regarding health and well-being.

2. Connection and Community: Technology facilitates social connections, allowing individuals to stay in touch with friends and family, join support groups, and engage with communities that share similar interests. This social connectivity can combat feelings of loneliness and isolation, which are crucial for emotional well-being.

3. Fitness and Health Monitoring: Fitness apps and wearable devices, such as fitness trackers, provide users with tools to monitor their physical activity, nutrition, and overall health. These technologies can motivate individuals to maintain a healthy lifestyle by tracking progress and setting fitness goals.

4. Telemedicine: The rise of telemedicine has transformed healthcare accessibility. Patients can consult healthcare professionals from the comfort of their homes, reducing the barriers to receiving medical advice and treatment. This convenience can lead to better health outcomes, especially for those with mobility issues or those living in remote areas.

Drawbacks of Excessive Screen Time

1. Physical Health Issues: Prolonged screen time is associated with various physical health problems, including eye strain, poor posture, and musculoskeletal disorders. The blue light emitted by screens can lead to digital eye strain, characterized by symptoms like dry eyes, blurred vision, and headaches. Additionally, sedentary behavior linked to excessive screen use can contribute to obesity, cardiovascular disease, and other chronic health conditions.

2. Mental Health Concerns: Studies have shown a correlation between excessive screen time and increased rates of anxiety, depression, and stress. The constant barrage of information and social media interactions can lead to feelings of inadequacy and comparison, negatively impacting self-esteem and overall mental health.

3. Sleep Disruption: Increased screen time, particularly before bedtime, can disrupt sleep patterns. The blue light emitted by screens interferes with the production of melatonin, a hormone that regulates sleep. Poor sleep quality can exacerbate other health issues, including cognitive function and emotional regulation.

4. Reduced Face-to-Face Interaction: While technology fosters online connections, it can also hinder real-life interactions. Excessive reliance on screens for communication may reduce opportunities for in-person socialization, which is vital for developing strong interpersonal relationships and emotional resilience.

Finding Balance

To mitigate the adverse effects of screen time while maximizing its benefits, it is essential to establish a balanced approach:

1. Set Time Limits: Designate specific times for screen use and prioritize activities that do not involve screens, such as exercise, reading, or spending time outdoors.

2. Create Tech-Free Zones: Designate areas in the home, such as the dining room or bedroom, as tech-free spaces to encourage face-to-face interaction and promote better sleep hygiene.

3. Prioritize Quality Content: Choose educational and uplifting content that contributes positively to your well-being. Engage with apps and platforms that foster connection and provide valuable information.

4. Practice Mindfulness: Be conscious of your screen time habits and their impact on your mood and energy levels. Regularly assess how screen use affects your physical health, mental state, and relationships.

By understanding the impacts of screen time on health and implementing strategies for balance, individuals can harness technology's advantages while minimizing its potential drawbacks. This approach promotes a healthier, more fulfilling lifestyle in an increasingly digital world.

Future Trends in Health Technology

As the landscape of health technology continues to rapidly evolve, several trends are emerging that promise to redefine how we approach health care, personal wellness, and disease prevention. These innovations aim to enhance patient outcomes, increase accessibility to health services, and empower individuals to take charge of their own health. Here are some of the most significant future trends in health technology:

1. Artificial Intelligence and Machine Learning

Artificial Intelligence (AI) and Machine Learning (ML) are poised to revolutionize healthcare by improving diagnostic accuracy, personalizing treatment plans, and predicting patient outcomes. AI algorithms can analyze vast amounts of data from medical records, imaging studies, and even genetic information to identify patterns that might not be visible to human practitioners. This technology can assist in early disease detection, such as identifying cancers in radiology images or predicting cardiovascular events, making it a powerful tool in preventive health care.

2. Telemedicine and Virtual Health Services

The COVID-19 pandemic accelerated the adoption of telemedicine, and this trend is expected to continue growing. Virtual health services provide patients with the ability to consult healthcare providers through video calls, reducing the need for in-person visits. This shift not only expands access to care, especially for individuals in rural or underserved areas, but also allows for greater flexibility in managing chronic conditions and follow-up appointments. Future advancements will likely include more integrated telehealth platforms that seamlessly connect patients with a range of health services.

3. Wearable Health Technology

Wearable devices, such as fitness trackers and smartwatches, have become increasingly popular in monitoring health metrics like heart rate, sleep patterns, and physical activity levels. The future of wearables lies in their ability to provide real-time health data that can be shared with healthcare providers. Innovations may include more advanced sensors capable of monitoring glucose levels, blood pressure, and even mental health indicators. This continuous stream of data can facilitate more personalized health interventions and timely medical responses.

4. Blockchain for Health Records

Blockchain technology has the potential to transform health information management by providing a secure, decentralized system for storing and sharing medical records. This approach can enhance data privacy, reduce the risk of breaches, and ensure that patients have control over their medical information. With blockchain, patients can grant access to their health records to different providers as needed, improving care coordination and reducing redundant testing.

5. Genomics and Personalized Medicine

Advancements in genomics are paving the way for personalized medicine, where treatments and preventive strategies are tailored to an individual's genetic makeup. As the cost of genomic sequencing continues to decrease, more individuals will have access to their genetic information, allowing for targeted therapies that are more effective and have fewer side effects. This trend will also enable proactive health management, as individuals can better understand their predisposition to certain diseases and take preventive measures.

6. Augmented and Virtual Reality

Augmented Reality (AR) and Virtual Reality (VR) are beginning to find applications in medical training, patient education, and even treatment. AR can create immersive experiences for medical students, allowing them to practice procedures in a simulated environment. For patients, VR can be a powerful tool for pain management and rehabilitation, offering distraction and engagement during recovery processes. As these technologies become more sophisticated and accessible, their role in healthcare will expand.

7. Health Data Interoperability

The future of health technology will also focus on improving interoperability—the ability of different health systems and technologies to communicate and share data effectively. Enhanced interoperability will lead to better care coordination, reduced medical errors, and a more comprehensive understanding of patient health across multiple providers and settings.

Conclusion

The future of health technology holds immense promise for improving individual health outcomes and transforming the healthcare system. As these innovations take shape, it is essential for stakeholders, including healthcare providers, patients, and policymakers, to embrace these changes and ensure that technology enhances the quality of care while prioritizing ethical considerations and patient privacy. The interplay between technology and health will continue to grow, offering exciting opportunities for a healthier future.

Chapter 12

Cultivating Healthy Habits

The Science of Habit Formation

Habits are powerful forces in our lives, shaping our daily routines and influencing our overall well-being. Understanding the science behind how habits are formed and maintained is essential for anyone looking to cultivate healthier behaviors and make lasting changes.

The Habit Loop

At the core of habit formation is the concept of the "habit loop," a neurological pattern that governs any habit. This loop consists of three key components: the cue, the routine, and the reward.

1. Cue: The cue is a trigger that initiates the habit. It can be anything from a specific time of day, an emotional state, an environmental factor, or a preceding action. For example, feeling tired after work might cue someone to reach for a sugary snack.

2. Routine: The routine is the behavior or action that follows the cue. This is the habitual response to the trigger. In our example, the routine is the act of consuming the snack.

3. Reward: This is the positive reinforcement that follows the routine, which helps the brain recognize the value of the habit. In this case, the immediate satisfaction and energy boost from the sugary snack reinforce the behavior, making it more likely to occur again in the future.

The Role of Repetition

Habits are formed through repetition. When a behavior is repeated consistently in response to a cue, neural pathways in the brain become strengthened, making the action increasingly automatic. This process is known as "neuroplasticity," where the brain adapts based on experiences and behaviors.

Research shows that it typically takes about 21 to 66 days for a new behavior to become a habit, depending on the complexity of the action and individual differences. This timeline emphasizes the importance of patience and persistence when trying to establish new habits.

The Importance of Environment

Our environment plays a critical role in shaping our habits. The cues that trigger our behaviors are often embedded in our surroundings. For instance, if you want to develop a habit of exercising regularly, placing your workout clothes in a visible location can serve as a cue to prompt the routine of working out. Conversely, an environment filled with junk food can perpetuate unhealthy eating habits.

To foster positive habits, it is beneficial to create an environment that supports your goals. This might involve decluttering your space, surrounding yourself with motivational reminders, or even choosing social circles that encourage healthier behaviors.

Strategies for Habit Maintenance

Once a habit is formed, maintaining it requires ongoing effort. Here are some effective strategies:

1. Set Clear Intentions: Clearly define what habit you want to establish or maintain. Setting specific, measurable goals helps provide clarity and purpose.

2. Use Accountability: Sharing your goals with friends or family can create a sense of accountability. Additionally, joining groups or communities with similar goals can provide support and encouragement.

3. Track Progress: Keeping a journal or utilizing apps to track your habits can help visualize your progress, which can be motivating. Celebrating small milestones along the way reinforces the behavior.

4. Implement Gradual Changes: Instead of attempting a complete overhaul of your lifestyle, introduce changes gradually. Start with small, manageable steps that can be built upon over time.

5. Practice Self-Compassion: Understand that setbacks are a natural part of the habit formation process. Practicing self-compassion and resilience helps you bounce back from challenges without losing sight of your goals.

Conclusion

The science of habit formation reveals that habits are not only automatic behaviors but also complex neurological processes influenced by cues, routines, and rewards. By understanding and applying these principles, individuals can cultivate healthier habits that lead to lasting changes in their lives. With intention, repetition, and an environment that supports growth, anyone can transform their routines and enhance their overall well-being.

Breaking Unhealthy Habits

Breaking unhealthy habits is a crucial step towards achieving a healthier lifestyle. Habits are deeply ingrained patterns of behavior that can be difficult to change, as they often operate on autopilot. However, with the right strategies and mindset, it is entirely possible to replace negative behaviors with positive ones. Here are some effective strategies to help you break unhealthy habits:

1. Identify the Triggers

The first step in breaking an unhealthy habit is to identify what triggers it. Triggers can be emotional, situational, or even environmental. Keep a journal to track when you engage in the behavior, what you were doing at the time, and how you felt. By pinpointing these triggers, you can develop strategies to avoid or manage them effectively. For example, if stress leads you to snack mindlessly, consider alternative coping mechanisms such as deep breathing, exercise, or journaling.

2. Set Clear Goals

Establishing clear and achievable goals is vital. Instead of vague goals like "I want to eat healthier," opt for specific, measurable objectives such as "I will eat at least five servings of fruits and vegetables each day." SMART goals (Specific, Measurable, Achievable, Relevant, Time-bound) can help you stay focused and motivated. Break larger goals into smaller, manageable tasks to avoid feeling overwhelmed.

3. Replace the Habit

One effective way to break an unhealthy habit is to replace it with a healthier one. This principle, often referred to as "habit substitution," involves recognizing the cue (trigger) and then consciously choosing an alternative behavior. For example, if you habitually reach for a sugary snack in the afternoon, replace it with a piece of fruit or a handful of nuts. Over time, the new behavior can become the default response to the trigger.

4. Use Positive Reinforcement

Rewarding yourself for making positive changes can bolster your commitment to breaking unhealthy habits. Create a system of rewards for yourself when you achieve specific milestones. This could be as simple as treating yourself to a movie, enjoying a spa day, or indulging in a favorite hobby. Positive reinforcement can create a sense of accomplishment and motivate you to stay on track.

5. Develop a Support System

Having a solid support network can significantly enhance your chances of success. Share your goals with friends, family, or a supportive community. Consider joining a group where members share similar goals, such as a fitness class or a health-focused online community. Mutual encouragement and accountability can help you stay motivated, especially during challenging times.

6. Practice Mindfulness

Mindfulness techniques can help you become more aware of your habits and the cravings that drive them. Mindfulness involves paying attention to the present moment without judgment. By practicing mindfulness, you can learn to observe your thoughts and feelings without immediately reacting to them, allowing you to make more conscious choices. Techniques such as meditation, deep breathing exercises, or yoga can foster mindfulness, making it easier to resist unhealthy habits.

7. Be Patient and Persistent

Breaking habits takes time, and setbacks are a natural part of the process. It's essential to be patient with yourself and recognize that change often involves trial and error. If you slip up, don't be discouraged; instead, analyze what happened and adjust your approach. Persistence is key—each small step towards breaking an unhealthy habit brings you closer to your overall health goals.

In conclusion, breaking unhealthy habits is a journey that requires self-awareness, commitment, and strategic action. By understanding your triggers, setting clear goals, replacing negative behaviors, reinforcing positive changes, seeking support, practicing mindfulness, and maintaining patience, you can successfully transform your habits into healthier ones. Embrace the process of change with an open mind, and celebrate your progress along the way.

Developing New Healthy Habits

Creating and maintaining healthy habits is a fundamental aspect of leading a balanced and fulfilling life. Healthy habits not only enhance physical well-being but also contribute positively to mental and emotional health. The journey of habit formation can be broken down into several key steps that facilitate the introduction of positive changes and ensure their sustainability over time.

1. Start Small and Specific

The first step in developing new healthy habits is to start with small, specific goals. Instead of attempting to overhaul your entire lifestyle overnight, focus on one behavior at a time. For instance, if you want to incorporate more physical activity into your routine, you might begin with a goal of taking a 10-minute walk each day. This approach minimizes feelings of overwhelm and makes it easier to integrate the new habit into your life.

2. Understand the 'Why'

Understanding the motivation behind your desire to change is crucial. Ask yourself why you want to adopt this new habit. Is it to improve your health, enhance your mood, or increase your energy levels? Writing down your reasons can reinforce your commitment and serve as a reminder during challenging times. By connecting emotionally with your goals, you create a stronger desire to stick with them.

3. Use the SMART Criteria

When setting your goals, consider using the SMART criteria—Specific, Measurable, Achievable, Relevant, and Time-bound. For example, instead of saying, "I want to eat healthier," you could say, "I will eat at least two servings of vegetables with dinner five times a week for the next month." This structured approach helps clarify your objectives and provides a clear framework for tracking your progress.

4. Establish Triggers and Routines

Habits are often built around triggers—cues that prompt you to engage in a behavior. Identify existing routines in your daily life that can serve as triggers for your new habits. For example, if you want to practice mindfulness, you could link it to your morning coffee ritual. After pouring your coffee, take five minutes to meditate. By associating your new habit with an established routine, you create a seamless transition that fosters consistency.

5. Monitor Your Progress

Keeping track of your progress is essential for habit formation. Use a journal, app, or habit-tracking tool to record your daily achievements. Monitoring not only provides a visual representation of your progress but also allows you to celebrate small victories, reinforcing your commitment. Regularly reviewing your successes and challenges can help you make necessary adjustments and keep you motivated.

6. Stay Flexible

While consistency is important, it's equally vital to remain flexible. Life can be unpredictable, and you may encounter obstacles that disrupt your routine. Rather than viewing setbacks as failures, treat them as learning opportunities. Reflect on what caused the interruption and adapt your strategies accordingly. Flexibility in your approach enables you to navigate challenges without losing sight of your goals.

7. Build a Support System

Having a support system can significantly enhance your ability to develop and sustain healthy habits. Share your goals with friends, family, or a community group, and seek encouragement and accountability. Joining a fitness class, participating in a wellness group, or engaging with online communities can provide additional motivation and support, making the journey more enjoyable.

8. Practice Self-Compassion

Finally, practice self-compassion throughout the process. Developing new habits can be challenging, and it's normal to encounter difficulties along the way. Be kind to yourself during setbacks and recognize that change takes time. Celebrate your progress, no matter how small, and remind yourself that every step taken towards a healthier lifestyle is a step worth acknowledging.

Conclusion

In summary, developing new healthy habits is a gradual process that requires commitment, reflection, and flexibility. By starting small, understanding your motivations, and creating a supportive environment, you can introduce and sustain positive changes that lead to a healthier, more fulfilling life. Remember, the journey of health is not a sprint but a marathon; embrace each step as part of your growth and well-being.

The Role of Motivation and Willpower

Motivation and willpower are fundamental components in the journey toward a healthier lifestyle. They not only drive individuals to set health-related goals but also empower them to persist in the face of challenges and obstacles. Understanding and harnessing these elements can significantly affect one's ability to implement and sustain healthy habits.

Understanding Motivation

Motivation can be broadly categorized into two types: intrinsic and extrinsic. Intrinsic motivation comes from within; it involves engaging in activities for their own sake, such as exercising because it makes you feel good or cooking healthy meals because you enjoy the process. Extrinsic motivation, on the other hand, is driven by external rewards or pressures, such as wanting to lose weight to fit into a certain dress size or to receive praise from others. Both types of motivation have their place, but intrinsic motivation tends to be more sustainable over the long term because it fosters a genuine connection to the activity itself.

Setting Clear Goals

A key strategy for enhancing motivation is to set clear, attainable goals. The SMART criteria—Specific, Measurable, Achievable, Relevant, and Time-bound—can help individuals formulate goals that are concrete and meaningful. For example, instead of setting a vague goal like "I want to be healthier," one might aim for "I will exercise for 30 minutes at least four times a week for the next month." This specificity not only clarifies what needs to be done but also provides a measurable benchmark for success.

Cultivating Willpower

Willpower, often referred to as self-control, is the ability to resist short-term temptations in order to meet long-term goals. It is a finite resource that can be strengthened through practice. Strategies to enhance willpower include:

1. Prioritizing Tasks: Understanding which habits are most crucial to your health journey and focusing your willpower on those can optimize your efforts.

2. Creating a Supportive Environment: Surrounding yourself with positive influences and removing temptations can help bolster willpower. For instance, keeping healthy snacks visible and accessible can make it easier to choose them over unhealthy options.

3. Mindfulness Practices: Engaging in mindfulness can improve self-awareness and help individuals recognize when they are being tempted by unhealthy behaviors. Techniques such as meditation or deep-breathing exercises can enhance focus and resilience.

Overcoming Obstacles

Obstacles are an inevitable part of any journey toward health. These may include time constraints, stress, lack of resources, or even social pressures. **To overcome these challenges, consider the following strategies:**

1. Anticipate Challenges: Prepare for potential setbacks by identifying common obstacles you may face. For example, if you know you tend to skip workouts when busy, plan shorter, more intense workout sessions for those times.

2. Develop a Flexible Mindset: Understand that setbacks are a normal part of any health journey. Instead of viewing them as failures, see them as opportunities to learn and adapt your approach.

3. Seek Support: Engaging with friends, family, or support groups can provide encouragement and accountability. Sharing your goals with others can increase motivation and help sustain commitment.

Celebrating Progress

Recognizing and celebrating small victories can significantly boost motivation. Whether it's completing a week of workouts or trying a new healthy recipe, taking time to acknowledge achievements reinforces positive behavior and enhances willpower. Consider keeping a journal to track progress and reflect on what worked well and what could be improved.

In conclusion, motivation and willpower are essential tools in the quest for a healthier lifestyle. By understanding the nature of motivation, cultivating willpower, preparing for obstacles, and celebrating progress, individuals can build a resilient framework that supports sustained healthy living. Embracing this journey as a series of small, manageable steps can make the process not only achievable but also enjoyable.

Tracking Progress and Celebrating Success

In the journey toward a healthier lifestyle, tracking progress and celebrating successes are essential components that can significantly enhance motivation, accountability, and overall satisfaction with the process. Monitoring improvements not only provides tangible evidence of your hard work but also fosters a positive mindset that encourages continued commitment to your health goals.

The Importance of Tracking Progress

Tracking progress serves multiple purposes, primarily allowing you to see the results of your efforts. Whether your goals are related to nutrition, physical activity, mental well-being, or any other aspect of health, having measurable indicators can help you understand what works and what might need adjustment. Here are several effective methods to monitor your health improvements:

1. Journaling: Keeping a health journal can provide insights into your daily habits, thoughts, and feelings. Documenting your meals, exercise routines, sleep patterns, and emotional states can help you identify trends and triggers. This practice also fosters mindfulness, making you more aware of your choices and their impacts.

2. Metrics and Measurements: Depending on your goals, you might track specific metrics, such as weight, body measurements, blood pressure, or fitness levels. Tools like fitness trackers or mobile apps can help you log workouts, calorie intake, and hydration. These quantitative measures can illustrate your progress over time and motivate you to stay on track.

3. Regular Health Assessments: Engaging in regular health screenings or assessments can offer a comprehensive view of your overall well-being. This could include routine check-ups with your healthcare provider, blood tests, or fitness evaluations. The feedback you receive can inform your health plan and highlight areas needing attention.

4. Setting Milestones: Break your larger health goals into smaller, achievable milestones. This approach not only makes goals more manageable but also provides multiple opportunities for celebration. Each time you reach a milestone, whether it's completing a certain number of workouts or sticking to a balanced diet for a specific period, take a moment to acknowledge your achievement.

Celebrating Successes

Celebrating successes, no matter how small, is crucial in maintaining motivation and reinforcing positive behaviors. Recognition of your hard work can build confidence and encourage you to continue striving for your goals. Here are some creative ways to celebrate your achievements:

1. Rewarding Yourself: Consider treating yourself to something special when you reach a goal. This could be a new workout outfit, a massage, or a day off to relax. Make sure that your rewards align with your health goals—celebrating with a healthy meal or a fun outdoor activity can reinforce positive behaviors.

2. Sharing Achievements: Sharing your progress with friends, family, or a support group can amplify the joy of your successes. Not only does this create a sense of accountability, but it also allows you to inspire others on their health journeys. Social media platforms can also be a venue for sharing your progress and receiving encouragement from your community.

3. Reflecting on Your Journey: Take time to reflect on how far you've come. Review your journal entries, photos, or any other documentation of your journey. Acknowledging your efforts and the changes you've made can reinforce your commitment and remind you why you started in the first place.

4. Revising Goals: After celebrating a success, consider setting new or adjusted goals. This keeps the momentum going and allows you to continually challenge yourself. Reassessing your goals ensures they remain relevant and aligned with your evolving health journey.

In conclusion, tracking progress and celebrating successes are vital practices in the pursuit of healthy living. By monitoring your improvements and recognizing your achievements, you cultivate a positive feedback loop that enhances motivation and encourages sustainable lifestyle changes. Embrace the journey, and remember that every step toward better health is worth celebrating!

Chapter 13

Holistic Health Approaches

What is Holistic Health?

Holistic health is a comprehensive approach to well-being that considers the interconnectedness of the body, mind, and spirit. Unlike conventional medicine, which often focuses on treating specific symptoms or diseases, holistic health emphasizes the importance of overall wellness and the balance between various aspects of an individual's life. The philosophy behind holistic health is that true well-being extends beyond just the absence of illness; it involves a harmonious state where physical, emotional, mental, and spiritual elements are in sync.

At the core of holistic health is the belief that every person is unique and that health is a personal journey. This perspective encourages individuals to take an active role in their well-being by recognizing their individual needs and circumstances. Holistic health practitioners often assess not just the physical state of a patient but also their emotional and psychological well-being, lifestyle choices, and spiritual beliefs. This broad perspective allows for a more tailored and effective approach to health care.

One of the key principles of holistic health is the idea that the body has an innate ability to heal itself. Holistic practitioners believe that by supporting the body's natural healing processes, individuals can achieve optimal health. This can involve a variety of practices, including proper nutrition, regular physical activity, stress management techniques, and mindfulness practices. By fostering an environment conducive to healing, individuals can often alleviate symptoms and improve their overall health without relying solely on pharmaceuticals or invasive procedures.

In addition to physical health, holistic health places significant emphasis on emotional and mental well-being. Mental health is recognized as a critical component of overall health, influencing how individuals think, feel, and behave. Holistic approaches often include techniques such as meditation, yoga, and counseling to help individuals manage stress, anxiety, and emotional turmoil. These practices support emotional resilience and encourage a positive mindset, which is vital for maintaining health.

Spiritual health is another dimension of holistic well-being. This aspect involves finding meaning, purpose, and connection in life, whether through religion, personal beliefs, or nature.

Engaging in spiritual practices can foster a sense of peace and fulfillment, which significantly contributes to overall well-being. Holistic health encourages individuals to explore their spirituality and integrate it into their daily lives, recognizing that spiritual health can influence physical and emotional health.

Furthermore, holistic health recognizes the impact of lifestyle choices on well-being. Diet, exercise, sleep, and social connections all play crucial roles in achieving balance and health. Holistic practitioners often advocate for a balanced diet rich in whole foods, regular physical activity tailored to the individual's preferences, sufficient sleep for recovery, and strong social networks for support. By addressing these lifestyle factors, individuals can create a healthier environment for themselves.

In summary, holistic health is a multidimensional approach that considers the whole person rather than just isolated symptoms or conditions. It emphasizes the importance of balance among physical, emotional, mental, and spiritual health, promoting the idea that optimal well-being comes from understanding and nurturing these interconnected aspects of life. By adopting a holistic perspective, individuals are empowered to take charge of their health, make informed choices, and cultivate a fulfilling and healthy life. Ultimately, holistic health encourages a proactive stance towards well-being, fostering resilience and harmony in the journey of life.

Integrating Mind, Body, and Spirit

In our pursuit of health and well-being, it is essential to recognize the interconnectedness of the mind, body, and spirit. Each component influences the others, and a holistic approach to health emphasizes the importance of nurturing all three in harmony. Achieving this balance requires self-awareness, intentional practices, and a commitment to integrating these aspects into daily life.

Understanding the Triad of Health

The mind encompasses our thoughts, emotions, and mental processes. Mental health is foundational to overall well-being; it influences how we cope with stress, relate to others, and make choices. The body represents our physical health, including nutrition, exercise, and sleep. Physical well-being is critical for sustaining energy and mobility, allowing us to engage fully in life. The spirit, often associated with our values, beliefs, and sense of purpose, provides meaning and direction. Nurturing the spirit fosters resilience, optimism, and a deeper connection to ourselves and others.

Creating Balance through Mindfulness

Mindfulness is a powerful practice for integrating mind, body, and spirit. It involves paying attention to the present moment without judgment, allowing us to connect more deeply with our experiences. Regular mindfulness practices, such as meditation, yoga, or mindful walking, can enhance self-awareness and reduce stress. By cultivating mindfulness, we can better understand our thoughts and emotions, recognize physical sensations in our bodies, and tap into our spiritual beliefs. This awareness helps us make healthier choices and respond to life's challenges with greater clarity and calmness.

Nurturing the Body for Mental and Spiritual Health

A balanced approach to health begins with caring for the body. Nutrition plays a crucial role in this process; a diet rich in whole foods—fruits, vegetables, lean proteins, and healthy fats—supports both physical health and cognitive function. Regular physical activity is equally important, as exercise releases endorphins that elevate mood and reduce anxiety. Additionally, incorporating practices such as deep breathing and stretching can help release physical tension and promote relaxation.

Sleep is another vital component of physical health that directly impacts mental and emotional well-being. Establishing a consistent sleep routine and creating a restful sleep environment can enhance sleep quality, leading to improved mood and mental clarity. When the body is well-cared for, it provides a solid foundation for mental and spiritual growth.

Exploring Spiritual Practices

Integrating the spiritual dimension into daily life can significantly enhance overall well-being. Spirituality is a personal journey and may involve religious beliefs, meditation, or connection with nature. Practices such as journaling, prayer, or engaging in community service can foster a sense of purpose and connection to something greater than oneself. Spending time in nature, for instance, allows for reflection and a deeper appreciation of life, which can nurture the spirit and contribute to emotional resilience.

Setting Intentions and Goals

To integrate mind, body, and spirit effectively, it is helpful to set intentions and goals that reflect your values and aspirations. Consider what balance means for you and identify specific practices that resonate. This might include daily meditation, regular physical activity, or engaging in creative outlets that inspire joy. By consciously setting these intentions, you create a roadmap for nurturing each aspect of your health.

Conclusion

Integrating mind, body, and spirit is a lifelong journey that requires awareness, commitment, and self-compassion. By embracing a holistic approach to health, we can cultivate a more balanced and fulfilling life. This integration fosters resilience, enhances our ability to cope with challenges, and ultimately leads to a profound sense of well-being. Through mindful practices, nurturing our bodies, and exploring our spiritual dimensions, we can create harmony within ourselves and thrive in all areas of life.

Alternative and Complementary Therapies

In the quest for holistic health and well-being, alternative and complementary therapies have gained recognition as valuable approaches that can enhance traditional medical treatments. These therapies focus on treating the individual as a whole, rather than just addressing specific symptoms or illnesses. This section will provide an overview of some prominent alternative and complementary therapies, including acupuncture, chiropractic care, and herbal medicine, examining their principles, potential benefits, and applications.

Acupuncture

Acupuncture is a traditional Chinese medicine practice that involves inserting thin needles into specific points on the body, known as acupuncture points. This ancient technique is based on the belief that energy, or "qi" (pronounced "chee"), flows through pathways in the body called meridians. When the flow of qi is disrupted, it can lead to pain and illness. By stimulating acupuncture points, practitioners aim to restore the balance of energy and promote healing.

Research has shown that acupuncture can be effective for managing various conditions, including chronic pain, migraines, anxiety, and stress. It is believed to work by triggering the body's natural painkillers, such as endorphins, and by affecting the nervous system, leading to a reduction in inflammation and improved blood flow. Many patients report feeling relaxed and rejuvenated after an acupuncture session, making it a popular choice for those seeking alternative methods to alleviate discomfort and enhance overall well-being.

Chiropractic Care

Chiropractic care is a healthcare discipline that focuses on diagnosing and treating musculoskeletal disorders, particularly those related to the spine. Chiropractors utilize manual manipulation techniques, known as spinal adjustments, to align the spine and improve the function of the nervous system. The underlying principle is that proper spinal alignment can influence overall health and well-being by enabling the body to heal itself.

Chiropractic care has been shown to be particularly beneficial for individuals suffering from back pain, neck pain, and headaches. Studies suggest that spinal manipulation can lead to significant improvements in pain levels and functional ability. In addition to adjustments, chiropractors may incorporate other therapies such as massage, exercise, and lifestyle counseling to create a comprehensive treatment plan tailored to each patient's needs. For many, chiropractic care offers a non-invasive alternative to pain medication and surgery.

Herbal Medicine

Herbal medicine, also known as botanical medicine, involves the use of plants and plant extracts for therapeutic purposes. This practice dates back thousands of years and is an integral part of various traditional healing systems worldwide, including Traditional Chinese Medicine and Ayurveda. Herbal remedies can be used to support health, prevent illness, and treat a range of conditions.

Herbs can be consumed in various forms, such as teas, tinctures, capsules, or topical applications. Commonly used herbs include ginger for digestive issues, turmeric for its anti-inflammatory properties, and echinacea for immune support. It is essential to approach herbal medicine with caution and to consult healthcare professionals, as some herbs can interact with prescription medications or have side effects.

Integrating Alternative Therapies

While alternative and complementary therapies can offer significant benefits, they should be viewed as part of a holistic approach to health rather than replacements for conventional medicine. Collaboration between healthcare providers and practitioners of alternative therapies can create a comprehensive health plan that addresses all aspects of an individual's well-being.

In conclusion, acupuncture, chiropractic care, and herbal medicine are just a few examples of the many alternative and complementary therapies available today. Each offers unique benefits and can contribute to a balanced approach to health. As with any health-related decision, it is crucial to conduct thorough research, seek qualified practitioners, and communicate openly with healthcare providers to ensure safe and effective use of these therapies. By integrating these approaches into a broader health strategy, individuals can work towards achieving optimal health and well-being.

The Role of Nutrition in Holistic Health

Nutrition is a cornerstone of holistic health, which emphasizes the interconnectedness of mind, body, and spirit. In holistic practices, diet is not merely about consuming the right foods; it encompasses a broader understanding of how what we eat affects our overall well-being. This comprehensive approach to nutrition recognizes that food can influence not only physical health but also mental and emotional states, thereby contributing to a balanced and fulfilled life.

Understanding Holistic Nutrition

Holistic nutrition goes beyond calorie counting and macronutrient ratios. It involves selecting foods that nourish the body at a cellular level while also considering the emotional and psychological aspects of eating. This means choosing whole, unprocessed foods that are rich in nutrients, rather than opting for convenience foods that may be laden with preservatives and artificial ingredients. Foods such as fresh fruits and vegetables, whole grains, lean proteins, and healthy fats play a crucial role in supporting bodily functions and maintaining energy levels.

Additionally, holistic nutrition emphasizes the importance of mindful eating practices. This includes being aware of hunger and fullness cues, which can foster a healthier relationship with food. Mindful eating encourages individuals to savor their meals, appreciating flavors and textures, which can enhance the overall eating experience and lead to greater satisfaction. This practice can also help in reducing emotional eating, as individuals become more attuned to their body's needs rather than using food as a coping mechanism.

The Impact of Nutrients on Overall Health

Different nutrients have specific roles that contribute to holistic health. For instance, antioxidants found in fruits and vegetables help to combat oxidative stress and inflammation, which are linked to numerous chronic diseases. Omega-3 fatty acids, prevalent in fish and flaxseeds, support brain health and can improve mood and cognitive function. Likewise, complex carbohydrates provide a steady source of energy that stabilizes blood sugar levels, which is crucial for maintaining mental clarity and emotional stability.

Furthermore, adequate hydration is often overlooked in discussions about nutrition, yet it is fundamental to holistic health. Water aids in digestion, nutrient absorption, and even the regulation of mood. Encouraging proper hydration is essential for maintaining optimal physiological functions and emotional well-being.

Integrating Dietary Practices into Holistic Health

When creating a personalized holistic health plan, it is vital to incorporate nutritional practices that resonate with individual lifestyles and preferences. This might involve exploring various dietary patterns, such as Mediterranean, plant-based, or anti-inflammatory diets, that align with holistic principles. Each of these diets offers unique benefits while emphasizing whole foods and nutrient density.

Moreover, holistic health encourages seasonal and local eating. Consuming foods that are in season and locally sourced not only enhances freshness and flavor but also promotes sustainability. This practice fosters a greater connection with the environment and the community, reinforcing the holistic philosophy of interdependence.

Conclusion

In essence, nutrition plays a vital role in holistic health by providing the necessary building blocks for physical vitality, emotional balance, and mental clarity. A well-rounded diet supports the body's natural healing processes, enhances mood, and fosters overall well-being. By adopting mindful eating practices and prioritizing nutrient-dense foods, individuals can cultivate a healthy relationship with food that nourishes not only the body but also the mind and spirit. Ultimately, nutrition is a powerful tool in the holistic health journey, encouraging individuals to take an active role in their well-being and to embrace a lifestyle that promotes harmony and balance.

Creating a Personal Holistic Health Plan

Designing a personal holistic health plan is an empowering process that enables individuals to address their health and well-being comprehensively. A holistic approach emphasizes the interconnectedness of the mind, body, and spirit, recognizing that each aspect influences the others. By taking the time to create a plan tailored to your unique needs, preferences, and circumstances, you can cultivate a more balanced and fulfilling life. Here's how to design a holistic health plan that works for you.

1. Self-Assessment

The first step in creating a personal holistic health plan is to conduct a thorough self-assessment. This involves reflecting on your current physical health, mental and emotional well-being, and spiritual life. Consider using a journal or worksheet to evaluate the following areas:

- **Physical Health:** Assess your diet, exercise routines, sleep quality, and any chronic conditions. Are you meeting your nutritional needs? How active are you?

- **Mental Health:** Reflect on your stress levels, coping mechanisms, and mental clarity. Are you feeling anxious or overwhelmed? Do you have effective strategies in place for managing stress?

- **Emotional Well-being:** Think about your emotional resilience, relationships, and support systems. How do you navigate challenges? Are you connected with others?

- **Spiritual Health:** Explore your beliefs, values, and sense of purpose. Do you have practices that help you connect with your spiritual self, such as meditation, nature walks, or community service?

This self-assessment will provide a foundation for identifying areas that require attention and improvement.

2. Set Clear Goals

Once you understand your current state, the next step is to set clear, achievable goals. These goals should encompass all aspects of your health and well-being. Aim for SMART goals—Specific, Measurable, Achievable, Relevant, and Time-bound. For example:

- **Physical Goal:** "I will exercise for at least 30 minutes, five days a week for the next three months."

- **Mental Goal:** "I will practice mindfulness meditation for 10 minutes every morning for four weeks."

- **Emotional Goal:** "I will reach out to a friend or family member for support at least once a week to strengthen my connections."

- **Spiritual Goal:** "I will spend one hour each week volunteering to connect with my community and enhance my sense of purpose."

3. Create an Action Plan

With your goals in place, develop a detailed action plan outlining how you will achieve them. This plan should include specific activities, resources, and timelines. For instance:

- **Physical:** Schedule workouts in your calendar, explore new activities (like yoga or swimming), and prepare healthy meals in advance.

- **Mental:** Allocate time each day for mindfulness practices, identify stress triggers, and develop coping strategies, such as deep breathing or journaling.

- **Emotional:** Plan regular check-ins with loved ones and engage in activities that promote social bonding, like joining a club or attending community events.

- **Spiritual:** Incorporate practices that resonate with you, such as meditation, prayer, or spending time in nature.

4. Monitor Your Progress

Tracking your progress is essential for maintaining motivation and accountability. Keep a health journal or use digital tools to log your activities, emotions, and any changes in your physical health. Regularly review your goals and adjust your action plan as needed based on your experiences and feedback from your body and mind.

5. Embrace Flexibility

A holistic health plan should not be rigid. Life circumstances can change, and so can your needs and priorities. Be open to adjusting your plan as you learn more about yourself and your journey. Celebrate your successes, no matter how small, and be compassionate with yourself during setbacks.

6. Seek Support

Lastly, consider enlisting the support of professionals, such as registered dietitians, mental health counselors, or fitness trainers, to help you on your journey. Engaging with a community of like-minded individuals can also provide encouragement, accountability, and shared experiences that enrich your holistic health plan.

By taking these steps, you can create a personal holistic health plan that nurtures every aspect of your being, leading to a more balanced and fulfilling life. Embrace the journey, and remember that health is a continuous process of growth and discovery.

Chapter 14

Success Stories and Case Studies

What is Self-Care?

Self-care is a multifaceted concept that encompasses the practices individuals engage in to maintain and enhance their physical, mental, and emotional well-being. At its core, self-care involves recognizing one's needs and proactively taking steps to meet them. This can range from basic daily routines, such as maintaining hygiene and eating nutritious meals, to more complex activities like seeking therapy or engaging in hobbies that promote joy and relaxation. The significance of self-care cannot be overstated, as it is instrumental in fostering resilience, preventing burnout, and promoting overall health.

The Dimensions of Self-Care

Self-care is often categorized into several key dimensions, each playing a crucial role in an individual's health:

1. Physical Self-Care: This dimension involves activities that promote physical well-being. Examples include regular exercise, maintaining a balanced diet, ensuring adequate sleep, and attending regular health check-ups. These practices help maintain bodily functions and prevent chronic diseases, thereby enhancing quality of life.

2. Emotional Self-Care: This aspect focuses on recognizing and managing one's emotions effectively. It includes practices such as journaling, engaging in creative activities, and seeking support from friends or professionals when needed. Emotional self-care helps individuals understand their feelings, cope with stress, and foster a positive mindset.

3. Mental Self-Care: Engaging in activities that stimulate the mind is crucial for mental health. This can involve reading, continuing education, or practicing mindfulness and meditation. Mental self-care is vital for cognitive function and can help mitigate anxiety and depression.

4. Social Self-Care: Building and maintaining healthy relationships is a critical component of self-care. This can include spending time with loved ones, joining community groups, or simply reaching out to friends. Strong social connections provide emotional support and a sense of belonging, which are essential for mental health.

5. Spiritual Self-Care: For many, spirituality plays a significant role in overall well-being. Spiritual self-care might include practices like meditation, prayer, or connecting with nature. Engaging in spiritual activities can provide a sense of purpose and inner peace.

The Importance of Self-Care

The significance of self-care in health and well-being is manifold:

1. Prevention of Burnout: In today's fast-paced world, the risk of burnout is high, especially among caregivers, professionals, and individuals juggling multiple responsibilities. Regular self-care practices can help mitigate stress and prevent burnout by allowing individuals to recharge and refresh.

2. Improved Physical Health: Engaging in self-care activities can lead to healthier lifestyle choices, which in turn reduce the risk of developing chronic health conditions like heart disease, diabetes, and obesity. This proactive approach to health can enhance longevity and improve quality of life.

3. Enhanced Mental Health: Self-care is intrinsically linked to mental health. Taking time for oneself can lead to reduced anxiety and depression, improved mood, and greater emotional stability. It creates a buffer against the stresses of daily life, promoting resilience.

4. Better Relationships: When individuals prioritize self-care, they are often better equipped to engage in positive interactions with others. By caring for themselves, they can approach relationships with more patience, understanding, and compassion.

5. Increased Productivity and Focus: Taking breaks and engaging in self-care can enhance focus and productivity. When individuals feel rested and rejuvenated, they are more efficient and effective in their daily tasks.

In conclusion, self-care is not merely a luxury but a necessity for maintaining health and well-being. It involves a conscious effort to nurture oneself across various dimensions, ultimately leading to a more balanced and fulfilling life. By understanding and implementing self-care practices, individuals can enhance their resilience and capacity to cope with life's challenges, paving the way for a healthier and more rewarding existence.

Incorporating Self-Care into Daily Life

Incorporating self-care into daily life is essential for maintaining overall well-being and fostering resilience against the stresses of modern living. While self-care is often perceived as an indulgent luxury, it is, in fact, a vital practice that enhances mental, emotional, and physical health. Here are practical tips to prioritize self-care in your everyday routine:

1. Start Small: Begin by integrating small self-care activities into your daily schedule. This could be as simple as enjoying a cup of tea in the morning, taking a five-minute stretch break, or stepping outside for fresh air. The key is to make self-care manageable and sustainable, allowing it to seamlessly fit into your existing routine.

2. Schedule Self-Care Time: Just as you would schedule a meeting or appointment, carve out dedicated time for self-care in your calendar. Whether it's a weekly yoga class, a daily walk, or a nightly reading session, treat this time as a non-negotiable commitment to yourself. Setting reminders can help reinforce this habit until it becomes a natural part of your day.

3. Create a Self-Care Ritual: Developing a self-care ritual can provide structure and consistency to your self-care practice. This could include a morning routine that incorporates mindfulness activities such as meditation or journaling, or a nighttime routine that involves winding down with a warm bath and calming music. Rituals help create a sense of anticipation and satisfaction, making self-care feel rewarding.

4. Listen to Your Body: Self-care is about tuning into your own needs and responding accordingly. Pay attention to how you feel physically and emotionally. If you're feeling fatigued, allow yourself to rest. If you're feeling overwhelmed, consider engaging in a calming activity, such as deep breathing or a short walk. Listening to your body enhances your ability to prioritize self-care effectively.

5. Set Boundaries: One of the most challenging aspects of self-care is learning to say no. Setting clear boundaries around your time and energy is crucial for protecting your well-being. This might involve limiting social commitments, reducing screen time, or delegating tasks at work or home. Communicate your boundaries to others, and don't feel guilty about prioritizing your health.

6. Engage in Activities You Love: Self-care should be enjoyable and fulfilling. Identify activities that bring you joy and make you feel rejuvenated. Whether it's painting, gardening, dancing, or reading, carve out time for these passions. Engaging in hobbies not only serves as a form of self-care but also fosters creativity and personal expression.

7. Connect with Others: Social connections are a vital aspect of self-care. Make an effort to reach out to friends and family, whether through a phone call, video chat, or in-person meet-up.

Sharing experiences, laughter, and support can significantly enhance your emotional well-being. Consider joining a group or community activity that aligns with your interests to foster new connections.

8. Practice Mindfulness: Mindfulness practices such as meditation, yoga, or simply being present during daily activities can enhance your self-care routine. Mindfulness encourages you to be aware of your thoughts and feelings without judgment, promoting a sense of calm and clarity. Regular mindfulness practice can reduce stress and improve overall mental health.

9. Reflect and Adjust: Regularly assess your self-care practices to ensure they meet your evolving needs. Set aside time for reflection, perhaps at the end of each week, to evaluate what worked well and what could be improved. Self-care is not a one-size-fits-all approach; be open to adjusting your practices as necessary.

10. Be Kind to Yourself: Finally, practice self-compassion. Understand that self-care is a journey, and it's okay to have days when you struggle to prioritize it. Treat yourself with kindness and patience, and recognize that every small step towards self-care is a positive move towards overall well-being.

Incorporating self-care into daily life is a commitment to nurturing your health and happiness. By making self-care a priority, you empower yourself to lead a more balanced and fulfilling life.

The Role of Self-Compassion in Self-Care

In the journey toward a healthier life, self-compassion emerges as a foundational pillar of effective self-care. Self-compassion, as defined by psychologist Kristin Neff, involves treating oneself with kindness, understanding, and acceptance, particularly in times of struggle or perceived failure. This practice is not merely indulgent; it is a critical component of emotional resilience and overall well-being.

Understanding Self-Compassion

Self-compassion is built on three core components: self-kindness, common humanity, and mindfulness. Self-kindness refers to being warm and understanding toward ourselves when we experience pain or failure, rather than being harshly self-critical. Common humanity emphasizes the recognition that suffering and personal inadequacy are part of the shared human experience—an acknowledgment that we are not alone in our struggles. Mindfulness entails maintaining a balanced awareness of one's thoughts and feelings without over-identifying with them, which allows for a more objective and compassionate perspective.

Why Self-Compassion Matters in Self-Care

Self-compassion plays a vital role in self-care for several reasons:

1. Reduction of Negative Emotions: When we practice self-compassion, we are less likely to fall into the trap of self-criticism and negative self-talk, which can lead to feelings of anxiety and depression. By treating ourselves with kindness, we create a buffer against these harmful emotions, fostering a more positive mental state that encourages healthy behaviors.

2. Increased Motivation: Contrary to the belief that self-criticism drives improvement, research has shown that self-compassion actually enhances motivation. When we are compassionate toward ourselves, we are more likely to approach challenges with an open heart and a willingness to learn, rather than retreating in fear of failure. This mindset encourages us to engage in self-care activities, knowing that we are worthy of care and love.

3. Enhanced Resilience: Self-compassion fosters resilience by allowing us to bounce back from setbacks. When we face challenges, being kind to ourselves helps us to process these experiences constructively, learning from them without becoming overwhelmed. This resilience is crucial in maintaining consistent self-care practices, as it empowers us to face obstacles without losing sight of our health goals.

4. Healthier Relationships: Practicing self-compassion not only benefits our relationship with ourselves but also enhances our relationships with others. When we are kind to ourselves, we are more likely to extend that same kindness to those around us. This creates a supportive environment where mutual care can thrive, further reinforcing our self-care efforts.

Cultivating Self-Compassion

To integrate self-compassion into your self-care routine, consider the following strategies:

- Practice Mindfulness: Take time to observe your thoughts and feelings with a non-judgmental attitude. Acknowledge your struggles without harsh criticism, allowing yourself to feel without the weight of judgment.

- Engage in Positive Self-Talk: Challenge negative thoughts by reframing them into compassionate statements. Instead of saying, "I can't believe I messed up again," try saying, "It's okay; everyone makes mistakes, and I can learn from this."

- **Write a Self-Compassion Letter:** When you're feeling down, write a letter to yourself as if you were writing to a close friend facing the same situation. Offer encouragement, understanding, and kindness.

- **Develop a Self-Care Ritual:** Incorporate practices that foster self-compassion into your daily routine. This might include meditation, journaling, or simply taking a moment to breathe and appreciate your efforts.

In conclusion, self-compassion is a powerful ally in self-care. By embracing kindness toward ourselves, we not only improve our mental and emotional health but also create a nurturing environment that promotes overall well-being. As you embark on your self-care journey, remember that being gentle with yourself is a strength, not a weakness, and it is essential to living a healthy, fulfilling life.

Self-Care for Mental Health

In today's fast-paced world, prioritizing mental health is crucial for overall well-being. Self-care for mental health encompasses various practices that individuals can adopt to enhance their emotional resilience, reduce stress, and promote a positive mindset. Engaging in self-care can significantly improve mental clarity and emotional stability, making it an essential component of a healthy lifestyle.

Understanding Self-Care for Mental Health

Self-care refers to the intentional actions individuals take to care for their physical, emotional, and mental health. When it comes to mental health, self-care practices help individuals recognize their feelings, manage stress, and build resilience against life's challenges. It's important to note that self-care is not a one-size-fits-all approach; what works for one person may not work for another. Therefore, exploring a variety of practices can help individuals find what resonates best with them.

Practices to Support Mental and Emotional Well-Being

1. Mindfulness and Meditation: Mindfulness involves being present in the moment and cultivating an awareness of thoughts and feelings without judgment. Practices such as meditation, deep breathing exercises, and yoga can significantly reduce anxiety and enhance emotional resilience. Regular mindfulness practice helps train the brain to focus on the present, reducing rumination on past events and worries about the future.

2. Physical Activity: Regular exercise is a powerful form of self-care that has profound effects on mental health. Engaging in physical activity releases endorphins, which are natural mood lifters. Whether it's a brisk walk, a dance class, or a workout at the gym, finding an enjoyable form of exercise can boost overall well-being and reduce symptoms of depression and anxiety.

3. Social Connections: Building and maintaining strong relationships is vital for mental health. Social support can alleviate feelings of loneliness and isolation, which are often detrimental to emotional well-being. Make a conscious effort to connect with friends and family, participate in community activities, or join support groups. Sharing experiences and feelings can provide both emotional relief and valuable perspectives.

4. Creative Expression: Engaging in creative activities such as art, music, writing, or crafting can serve as an effective outlet for emotions. Creativity allows individuals to express feelings that might be difficult to articulate verbally. Whether it's through painting, journaling, or playing an instrument, creative expression can enhance self-awareness and promote healing.

5. Setting Boundaries: Learning to say "no" and setting healthy boundaries is an important aspect of self-care. Overcommitting can lead to burnout and feelings of being overwhelmed. Evaluate your responsibilities and prioritize what truly matters, allowing for time to recharge and engage in activities that bring joy and fulfillment.

6. Adequate Sleep: Sleep is crucial for mental health. Lack of sleep can exacerbate stress, anxiety, and depression. Establishing a consistent sleep routine, creating a restful environment, and practicing good sleep hygiene can significantly improve sleep quality. Aim for 7-9 hours of restorative sleep each night.

7. Seeking Professional Help: While self-care practices are beneficial, it's essential to recognize when professional help is needed. Therapy or counseling can provide valuable tools and strategies for managing mental health challenges. Mental health professionals can offer guidance, support, and a safe space to explore feelings.

Conclusion

Incorporating self-care practices into daily life can foster better mental health and emotional resilience. The key is to find activities that resonate personally and to make them a regular part of your routine. Remember, self-care is not selfish; it is an essential investment in your overall well-being. By prioritizing mental health through intentional self-care, individuals can navigate life's challenges with greater ease and maintain a healthier, more balanced lifestyle.

Overcoming Barriers to Self-Care

In today's fast-paced world, prioritizing self-care can feel like an insurmountable challenge. With the demands of work, family, and social obligations, the concept of taking time for oneself often gets pushed to the back burner. However, understanding and overcoming the barriers to self-care is crucial for maintaining overall health and well-being. By addressing these challenges head-on, individuals can cultivate a consistent self-care routine that fosters resilience and balance.

Identifying Common Barriers

The first step in overcoming barriers to self-care is identifying what stands in the way. Common obstacles include:

1. Time Constraints: Many people feel they lack the time to engage in self-care activities. Work commitments, family responsibilities, and social obligations can create a perception that there is simply no time left for personal well-being.

2. Guilt: Individuals may experience guilt when prioritizing their own needs over those of others. This can be particularly pronounced for caregivers or those in demanding roles, where the expectation to always be available for others is prevalent.

3. Lack of Resources: Some may believe they cannot afford self-care, whether financially or in terms of access to facilities like gyms, spas, or wellness centers. This mindset can lead to the misconception that self-care requires monetary investment or specific resources.

4. Perfectionism: The desire to do things perfectly can hinder individuals from starting or maintaining a self-care routine. This can manifest as an all-or-nothing mentality, where one feels that if they can't dedicate several hours to self-care, they might as well not engage in it at all.

5. Social Expectations: Cultural norms and societal pressures can reinforce the idea that self-care is selfish or indulgent. The belief that one should always be productive can prevent individuals from recognizing the importance of self-care as a necessity rather than a luxury.

Strategies for Overcoming Barriers

Once barriers have been identified, it's essential to implement strategies to overcome them:

1. Time Management: Start by scheduling self-care into your calendar. Treat it like any other appointment, allocating even just 10-15 minutes a day for activities that recharge you, such as reading, meditating, or taking a short walk. By consciously blocking out time for self-care, it becomes part of your routine rather than an afterthought.

2. Reframing Guilt: Shift the narrative around self-care by recognizing that taking care of yourself enables you to be more present and effective for others. Understand that self-care is not a selfish act but rather a necessary component of being able to care for loved ones and fulfill responsibilities.

3. Finding Affordable Options: Self-care doesn't have to be expensive. Explore low-cost or free activities that promote well-being, such as yoga sessions at home, nature walks, or journaling. There are numerous online resources offering guided meditations, workouts, and wellness advice that require no financial commitment.

4. Embracing Imperfection: Allow yourself to engage in self-care activities without the need for perfection. It's okay if your self-care routine looks different each day—what matters is the intention behind it. Start small and be flexible in your approach, focusing on progress rather than perfection.

5. Challenging Social Norms: Educate yourself about the benefits of self-care and share this knowledge with others. Engaging in conversations about the importance of well-being can help dispel myths surrounding self-care as a selfish act. Surround yourself with supportive individuals who understand your commitment to prioritizing your health.

Conclusion

Overcoming barriers to self-care is a vital step towards achieving and maintaining overall wellness. By recognizing the challenges, implementing practical strategies, and rethinking the societal narratives surrounding self-care, individuals can prioritize their own health. Remember, self-care is not an indulgence; it is a fundamental aspect of a balanced and fulfilling life. Taking the time to nurture oneself ultimately leads to greater resilience, improved mental and emotional well-being, and a more harmonious existence.

Chapter 15

Conclusion and Moving Forward

Recap of Key Takeaways

In the journey towards adopting a healthier lifestyle, several pivotal concepts emerge throughout 'A Healthy Living Book.' These key takeaways encapsulate the essence of healthy living, serving as a foundation for individuals seeking to enhance their overall well-being.

Understanding Healthy Living: At its core, healthy living encompasses a holistic approach that integrates physical, mental, and emotional health. It is crucial to define what a healthy life means, recognizing that it varies for each individual. By debunking common misconceptions about health, such as the belief that fitness is solely about weight loss or that mental health issues signify weakness, readers can foster a more inclusive understanding of health.

Nutrition Fundamentals: Nutrition plays a vital role in maintaining health, with a clear understanding of macronutrients (carbohydrates, proteins, and fats) and micronutrients (vitamins and minerals) being essential for creating a balanced diet. The importance of hydration cannot be overstated; water intake significantly impacts bodily functions and overall health. Readers are encouraged to learn how to interpret food labels and engage in meal planning to facilitate consistent healthy eating.

The Power of Physical Activity: Regular exercise is not merely a means to an end; it is a multifaceted tool that enhances physical, mental, and emotional well-being. Different types of physical activity, including aerobic, strength, flexibility, and balance exercises, contribute uniquely to health. Developing a sustainable fitness plan, recognizing barriers to exercise, and understanding the importance of rest and recovery are crucial aspects of maintaining an active lifestyle.

Mental and Emotional Well-Being: Mental health is a cornerstone of overall health, impacting every facet of life. Effective stress management techniques, the cultivation of a positive mindset, and the development of emotional resilience are key strategies for enhancing mental well-being. Mindfulness and meditation practices provide valuable tools for grounding oneself and promoting emotional health.

Quality Sleep: Sleep is foundational to health, with understanding sleep cycles and the consequences of sleep deprivation being critical for optimal functioning. Establishing a sleep-friendly environment and routine can significantly improve sleep quality, while recognizing and addressing sleep disorders is essential for long-term health.

Healthy Relationships: Social connections profoundly impact health. Building strong relationships, establishing boundaries, and managing conflict are all essential for nurturing mental and emotional health. Furthermore, the role of community in fostering well-being highlights the importance of social ties and support systems.

Work-Life Balance: Achieving a balance between work and personal life is crucial for maintaining health. Strategies for managing time, recognizing signs of burnout, and engaging in leisure activities support a healthy lifestyle. Maintaining balance during life changes ensures resilience during transitions.

Preventive Health: Preventive measures are vital in maintaining long-term health, emphasizing the adage that prevention is better than cure. Regular health screenings and vaccinations, along with personalized health plans, empower individuals to take charge of their health proactively.

Environmental Influences: The environment plays a significant role in health. Creating a healthy home, reducing exposure to toxins, and embracing nature contribute to overall well-being. Sustainable living practices not only benefit personal health but also promote a healthier planet.

Holistic Health and Self-Care: A holistic approach to health integrates mind, body, and spirit, recognizing the interconnectedness of various health aspects. Self-care, encompassing practices that prioritize mental, emotional, and physical well-being, is essential for maintaining balance in life.

Commitment to a Healthy Lifestyle: Ultimately, the journey towards health is ongoing. Developing a personal health plan, setting realistic goals, and committing to long-term lifestyle changes are critical for sustained success. Continuing education about health and wellness ensures individuals remain informed and inspired on their journey.

In conclusion, 'A Healthy Living Book' serves as a comprehensive guide, empowering readers to take actionable steps towards a healthier, more balanced life. By embracing these key takeaways, individuals can cultivate habits that enhance their overall well-being, paving the way for a fulfilling life.

Developing a Personal Health Plan

Creating a personal health plan is a crucial step towards achieving and maintaining a healthy lifestyle. A well-structured health plan not only provides direction but also serves as a roadmap for your health goals. It encompasses various aspects of health, including nutrition, physical activity, mental well-being, and preventive measures. Here are the key steps to develop and implement a comprehensive health plan tailored to your individual needs.

Step 1: Assess Your Current Health Status

Before you can create an effective health plan, it's essential to assess your current health status. Take note of your physical condition, including weight, fitness level, and any existing health issues. Consider scheduling a check-up with a healthcare professional to get a thorough evaluation. This can include blood tests, screenings, and discussions about your medical history. Understanding your baseline health will help you set realistic and achievable goals.

Step 2: Define Your Health Goals

Once you have a clear understanding of your health status, it's time to set specific, measurable, achievable, relevant, and time-bound (SMART) goals. These goals should reflect what you want to achieve in different areas of your health. For instance, you might aim to lose a certain amount of weight, increase your physical activity to a specific level, improve your dietary habits, or manage stress more effectively. Clearly defined goals will provide motivation and a sense of purpose as you work towards achieving them.

Step 3: Educate Yourself

Knowledge is a powerful tool in creating a successful health plan. Educate yourself about nutrition, exercise, mental health, and preventive care. Read reputable health literature, attend workshops, or consult with healthcare professionals and nutritionists. Understanding the principles of good health will empower you to make informed decisions and adjustments to your lifestyle.

Step 4: Develop Actionable Strategies

With your goals in mind, outline actionable strategies that will lead you to success. This may include:

- **Nutrition:** Plan balanced meals incorporating a variety of fruits, vegetables, whole grains, lean proteins, and healthy fats. Consider meal prepping to streamline your efforts.
- **Physical Activity:** Create a fitness routine that includes a mix of cardiovascular, strength training, and flexibility exercises. Aim for at least 150 minutes of moderate aerobic activity per week, as recommended by health guidelines.

- Mental Well-being: Incorporate stress management techniques such as mindfulness, meditation, or yoga. Schedule regular time for relaxation and hobbies that bring you joy.
- Preventive Health: Keep track of necessary screenings and vaccinations, and schedule regular check-ups to monitor your health.

Step 5: Create a Schedule

A practical health plan requires a schedule that integrates your new habits into your daily routine. Use a planner or digital calendar to block out time for meal preparation, workouts, and self-care activities. Consistency is key, so try to make these appointments non-negotiable, just as you would for work obligations or personal appointments.

Step 6: Monitor Your Progress

Regularly evaluate your progress towards your health goals. This can be done through journaling, using health apps, or maintaining a progress chart. Reflect on what's working and what isn't. Be flexible and willing to adjust your plan as needed. Celebrate small victories to keep yourself motivated, and don't hesitate to seek support from friends, family, or health professionals when facing challenges.

Step 7: Stay Committed and Adapt

Commitment to your health plan is vital for long-term success. Life can bring unexpected changes, and it's important to adapt your plan as necessary while staying focused on your overall health goals. Regularly revisit your plan, reassess your goals, and make adjustments to ensure that your personal health plan remains relevant and effective.

By following these steps, you can develop and implement a comprehensive personal health plan that not only addresses your current needs but also helps you cultivate a sustainable, healthy lifestyle for the future.

Staying Committed to a Healthy Lifestyle

Maintaining a healthy lifestyle is a journey rather than a destination. Commitment to this journey requires intentionality and resilience. Here are several strategies that can help you stay committed and sustain your healthy habits over the long term.

1. Set Realistic Goals

Begin by setting achievable and realistic health goals. Rather than striving for perfection, focus on incremental changes that are sustainable. For example, instead of committing to an intense workout regimen every day, aim for three to four sessions per week. Establishing small, attainable goals not only boosts your motivation but also reinforces your progress, making the journey less overwhelming.

2. Create a Support System

Surround yourself with individuals who support your health goals. This could be family, friends, or even online communities. Sharing your goals with others creates accountability and encouragement. Consider joining fitness classes, clubs, or online forums where you can connect with like-minded individuals. Having a support system can help you navigate challenges, celebrate successes, and maintain motivation.

3. Develop a Routine

Incorporating healthy habits into your daily routine can help solidify them as part of your lifestyle. Schedule your workouts, meal prep, and self-care activities just as you would any other important appointment. Consistency is key; by embedding these practices into your routine, they become second nature over time.

4. Monitor Your Progress

Tracking your progress can be a powerful motivator. Use journals, apps, or fitness trackers to log your daily activities, meals, and feelings. Regularly reviewing your progress helps you identify patterns, recognize accomplishments, and adjust your goals as needed. Celebrating milestones, no matter how small, can reinforce your commitment and provide a sense of achievement.

5. Stay Flexible and Adaptable

Life is unpredictable, and it's essential to remain flexible in your approach to healthy living. There will be times when your schedule is disrupted, or when unforeseen circumstances arise. Rather than viewing these as setbacks, embrace them as opportunities to adapt your plan. If you miss a workout, focus on maintaining balanced nutrition or try a shorter workout. Flexibility allows you to navigate changes without abandoning your overall commitment to health.

6. Educate Yourself Continuously

Knowledge is a powerful tool for maintaining commitment to a healthy lifestyle. Stay informed about nutrition, fitness, and mental well-being through books, podcasts, workshops, and reputable online resources. The more you know, the better equipped you will be to make informed choices that align with your health goals. Continuous learning can also reignite your passion for health as you discover new strategies and insights.

7. Prioritize Self-Care

Self-care is essential for long-term health. It's important to not only focus on physical health but also on mental and emotional well-being. Engage in activities that bring you joy, relaxation, and fulfillment. Whether that's practicing mindfulness, enjoying a hobby, or spending time in nature, self-care replenishes your energy and reinforces your commitment to a healthy lifestyle.

8. Practice Self-Compassion

Lastly, be kind to yourself throughout your journey. Understand that setbacks are a natural part of growth and that perfection is unattainable. Instead of criticizing yourself for perceived failures, practice self-compassion. Reflect on your experiences, learn from them, and move forward with a renewed sense of purpose.

In conclusion, staying committed to a healthy lifestyle requires a multifaceted approach that encompasses goal setting, support systems, routines, monitoring, flexibility, education, self-care, and self-compassion. By integrating these strategies into your daily life, you can cultivate lasting habits that enhance your overall well-being and foster a sustainable, healthy lifestyle. Remember, the journey is just as important as the destination; embrace it with patience and enthusiasm.

Resources for Continued Learning

Embarking on a journey toward healthier living is a lifelong commitment that evolves with time, knowledge, and experience. To support you in this endeavor, a wealth of resources is available that can deepen your understanding, enhance your skills, and keep you motivated. Below, we present a curated list of recommended books, websites, and tools that can serve as valuable companions on your path to a healthier life.

Recommended Books

1. "How Not to Die" by Dr. Michael Greger

This book provides evidence-based insights into the role of nutrition in preventing and reversing disease. Dr. Greger offers practical advice on how to incorporate plant-based foods into your diet for optimal health.

2. "The Power of Habit" by Charles Duhigg

Understanding habit formation is crucial for making lasting lifestyle changes. Duhigg explores the science behind habits and provides actionable strategies for breaking unhealthy patterns and developing positive ones.

3. "Mindfulness for Beginners" by Jon Kabat-Zinn

This accessible introduction to mindfulness and meditation offers techniques for reducing stress and improving mental well-being, making it an essential resource for anyone looking to enhance their emotional health.

4. "The 7 Habits of Highly Effective People" by Stephen R. Covey

Covey's classic work focuses on personal and professional effectiveness, providing timeless principles that can help you balance various aspects of life, including work and relationships.

5. "Why We Sleep" by Matthew Walker

This comprehensive exploration of sleep examines its critical role in health and well-being. Walker discusses practical tips for improving sleep quality and understanding sleep's impact on physical and mental health.

Informative Websites

1. ChooseMyPlate.gov

This website, maintained by the U.S. Department of Agriculture, offers resources on nutrition, including dietary guidelines, meal planning, and educational materials to help you build a balanced diet.

2. MentalHealth.gov

A government resource dedicated to providing information about mental health issues, this site offers guidance on managing stress, understanding mental health conditions, and finding support.

3. Mayo Clinic

The Mayo Clinic's website provides a wealth of information on various health topics, including preventive care, healthy living tips, and the latest research in health. It is a trusted source for accurate and up-to-date health information.

4. The Centers for Disease Control and Prevention (CDC)

The CDC offers a wide range of resources on health topics, including nutrition, physical activity, sleep, and mental health. Their extensive library of information can help you stay informed about public health recommendations.

5. NIA.nih.gov (National Institute on Aging)

This site provides valuable resources on aging, including health tips for older adults, information on cognitive health, and research findings relevant to maintaining a healthy lifestyle as you age.

Tools and Apps

1. MyFitnessPal
This popular app helps users track their nutrition and exercise, providing insights into dietary habits and calories consumed. It's an excellent tool for those looking to maintain a balanced diet and stay accountable.

2. Headspace
A mindfulness and meditation app that offers guided sessions to help reduce stress and improve mental well-being. Headspace is a great starting point for beginners looking to incorporate mindfulness into their daily routine.

3. Fitbit or Apple Health
Wearable technology such as Fitbit or the Apple Health app can help you monitor your physical activity, heart rate, and sleep patterns. These tools provide valuable feedback that can motivate you to stay active and healthy.

4. Sleep Cycle
This app tracks your sleep patterns and uses smart alarms to wake you up at the optimal time, ensuring you feel refreshed. It's a great resource for anyone looking to improve their sleep quality.

5. Evernote
While not health-specific, Evernote can be a valuable tool for organizing your health journey. You can track your meals, exercise routines, and even set reminders for self-care practices.

Final Thoughts
Continued learning is essential for maintaining and enhancing your healthy lifestyle. By utilizing these books, websites, and tools, you can stay informed, inspired, and empowered as you navigate your health journey. Remember, every small step counts, and investing in your knowledge is a powerful way to achieve lasting change.

Final Words of Encouragement
As we conclude this journey through 'A Healthy Living Book', it's essential to take a moment to reflect on the invaluable insights and practical strategies shared in the preceding chapters. Embracing a healthy lifestyle is not merely a temporary commitment; it is a dynamic, lifelong journey that evolves with you, adapting to your changing needs and circumstances. The

motivation to pursue health and well-being can often wane, but here are some encouraging thoughts to inspire and sustain your commitment to healthy living.

Firstly, remember that every small step counts. Health is not defined by grand gestures or overnight transformations. It is built through consistent, incremental changes. Whether it's choosing a nutritious snack, going for a short walk, or dedicating a few minutes to meditate, these small actions accumulate, leading to significant improvements in your overall health. Embrace each step as a victory, and celebrate your progress, no matter how minor it may seem.

Moreover, cultivate a mindset of self-compassion. The road to healthy living is often paved with challenges and setbacks. There may be days when you falter, when your motivation dips, or when life's demands threaten to derail your efforts. During these moments, it's crucial to treat yourself with kindness rather than criticism. Acknowledge that imperfection is part of being human, and instead of focusing on what went wrong, redirect your energy toward what you can do moving forward. Self-compassion fosters resilience, allowing you to bounce back stronger and more determined.

In addition, surround yourself with a supportive community. The people you choose to connect with can significantly impact your health journey. Seek out friends, family, or groups who share your commitment to healthy living, as they can offer encouragement, accountability, and inspiration. Engaging with others creates a sense of belonging and support, making the pursuit of health a shared experience rather than a solitary endeavor.

Set realistic and meaningful goals that resonate with your values and aspirations. Goals provide direction and purpose, but they should be achievable and personally significant. Instead of fixating solely on outcomes, such as weight loss or fitness levels, focus on the process and the experience. Define what healthy living means to you—whether it's feeling more energetic, improving your mental clarity, or simply enjoying life more fully. This personalized approach can fuel your motivation and make the journey more fulfilling.

As you move forward, prioritize lifelong learning. The field of health and wellness is continuously evolving, and staying informed will empower you to make better decisions for your health. Seek out books, podcasts, and workshops that resonate with your interests and expand your understanding of healthy living. This commitment to education not only enhances your knowledge but also ignites a passion for health that can sustain you over the long run.

Lastly, embrace the journey rather than rush toward the destination. Healthy living is a lifestyle, not a checklist. Engage with each aspect of your well-being—nutrition, physical activity, mental health, sleep, relationships, and self-care—mindfully and joyfully. Acknowledge that every day is an opportunity to learn, grow, and improve. The more present you are in the process, the more fulfilling and rewarding your health journey will be.

In closing, remember that you have the power to create a vibrant, healthy life. Take what you've learned, integrate it into your daily routine, and remain committed to your well-being. Every choice you make is a step toward a healthier future. Embrace the journey with open arms, and let your commitment to healthy living transform not only your life but also the lives of those around you. You are capable, you are worthy, and your health is your greatest treasure. Keep striving, keep learning, and most importantly, keep living well.